OLD GORGON GRAHAM

More Letters from a
Self-Made Merchant to His Son

By

GEORGE
HORACE LORIMER

Illustrations By

F.R. GRUGER

and

B. MARTIN JUSTICE

First published in 1903

British Library Cataloguing-in-Publication Data
A catalogue record for this book is available
from the British Library

FROM A SON
TO HIS FATHER

Contents

George Horace Lorimer 7

I. 9

II. 21

III. 27

IV. 37

V. 46

VI. 54

VII. 65

VIII. 75

IX. 84

X. 93

XI. 104

XII. 114

XIII. 122

XIV. 132

ILLUSTRATIONS

"We'll make the young people's society ride this
rooster out of town on a rail"........................... 17

"That's it—good lard gone wrong"....................... 41

"Tried to bust your poor old father" 62

Crying into her third plate of ice cream 66

"N-n-nothin' but a drink of water" 73

Exchanging the grip of the third degree 86

I don't really need a tarpon ... but I need a burned neck
and a peeled nose.................................... 105

"Say, Mr. Graham, don't you want that suit of
clothes back?" 120

GEORGE HORACE LORIMER

Who makes Saturday evening a big night

"Business is like oil −
it won't mix with anything but business"

"Education will broaden a narrow mind,
but there's no known cure for a big head"

"Appearances are deceitful, I know,
but so long as they are, there's nothing
like having them decieve for us instead of against us. "

I.

_____

From John Graham, head of the house of Graham &
Company, pork packers, in Chicago, familiarly known on
'Change as Old Gorgon Graham, to his son, Pierrepont, at
the Union Stock Yards.

*The old man is laid up temporarily for repairs, and Pier-
repont has written asking if his father doesn't feel that he is
qualified now to relieve him of some of the burden of active
management.*

CARLSBAD, October 4, 189-.

Dear Pierrepont: I'm sorry you ask so many questions that you
haven't a right to ask, because you put yourself in the position of
the inquisitive bull-pup who started out to smell the third rail on
the trolley right-of-way—you're going to be full of information
in a minute.

In the first place, it looks as if business might be pretty good
this fall, and I'm afraid you'll have your hands so full in your
place as assistant manager of the lard department that you won't
have time to run my job, too.

Then I don't propose to break any quick-promotion records
with you, just because you happened to be born into a job with
the house. A fond father and a fool son hitch up into a bad
team, and a good business makes a poor family carryall. Out of
business hours I like you better than any one at the office, but in
them there are about twenty men ahead of you in my affections.
The way for you to get first place is by racing fair and square, and

9

not by using your old daddy as a spring-board from which to jump over their heads. A man's son is entitled to a chance in his business, but not to a cinch.

It's been my experience that when an office begins to look like a family tree, you'll find worms tucked away snug and cheerful in most of the apples. A fellow with an office full of relatives is like a sow with a litter of pigs—apt to get a little thin and peaked as the others fat up. A receiver is next of kin to a business man's relatives, and after they are all nicely settled in the office they're not long in finding a job for him there, too. I want you to get this firmly fixed in your mind, because while you haven't many relatives to hire, if you ever get to be the head of the house, you'll no doubt marry a few with your wife.

For every man that the Lord makes smart enough to help himself, He makes two who have to be helped. When your two come to you for jobs, pay them good salaries to keep out of the office. Blood is thicker than water, I know, but when it's the blood of your wife's second cousin out of a job, it's apt to be thicker than molasses—and stickier than glue when it touches a good thing. After you have found ninety-nine sound reasons for hiring a man, it's all right to let his relationship to you be the hundredth. It'll be the only bad reason in the bunch.

I simply mention this in passing, because, as I have said, you ain't likely to be hiring men for a little while yet. But so long as the subject is up, I might as well add that when I retire it will be to the cemetery. And I should advise you to anchor me there with a pretty heavy monument, because it wouldn't take more than two such statements of manufacturing cost as I have just received from your department to bring me back from the graveyard to the Stock Yards on the jump. And until I do retire you don't want to play too far from first base. The man at the bat will always strike himself out quick enough if he has forgotten how to find the pitcher's curves, so you needn't worry about that. But you want to be ready all the time in case he should bat a few hot ones in your direction.

Some men are like oak leaves—they don't know when they're dead, but still hang right on; and there are others who let go before anything has really touched them. Of course, I may be in the first class, but you can be dead sure that I don't propose to get into the second, even though I know a lot of people say I'm an old hog to keep right along working after I've made more money than I know how to spend, and more than I could spend if I knew how. It's a mighty curious thing how many people think that if a man isn't spending his money their way he isn't spending it right, and that if he isn't enjoying himself according to their tastes he can't be having a good time. They believe that money ought to loaf; I believe that it ought to work. They believe that money ought to go to the races and drink champagne; I believe that it ought to go to the office and keep sober.

When a man makes a specialty of knowing how some other fellow ought to spend his money, he usually thinks in millions and works for hundreds. There's only one poorer hand at figures than these over-the-left financiers, and he's the fellow who inherits the old man's dollars without his sense. When a fortune comes without calling, it's apt to leave without asking. Inheriting money is like being the second husband of a Chicago grass-widow—mighty uncertain business, unless a fellow has had a heap of experience. There's no use explaining when I'm asked why I keep on working, because fellows who could put that question wouldn't understand the answer. You could take these men and soak their heads overnight in a pailful of ideas, and they wouldn't absorb anything but the few loose cuss-words that you'd mixed in for flavoring. They think that the old boys have corralled all the chances and have tied up the youngsters where they can't get at them; when the truth is that if we all simply quit work and left them the whole range to graze over, they'd bray to have their fodder brought to them in bales, instead of starting out to hunt the raw material, as we had to. When an ass gets the run of the pasture he finds thistles.

I don't mind owning up to you, though, that I don't hang on

because I'm indispensable to the business, but because business is indispensable to me. I don't take much stock in this indispensable man idea, anyway. I've never had one working for me, and if I had I'd fire him, because a fellow who's as smart as that ought to be in business for himself; and if he doesn't get a chance to start a new one, he's just naturally going to eat up yours. Any man can feel reasonably well satisfied if he's sure that there's going to be a hole to look at when he's pulled up by the roots.

I started business in a shanty, and I've expanded it into half a mile of factories; I began with ten men working for me, and I'll quit with 10,000; I found the American hog in a mud-puddle, without a beauty spot on him except the curl in his tail, and I'm leaving him nicely packed in fancy cans and cases, with gold medals hung all over him. But after I've gone some other fellow will come along and add a post-graduate course in pork packing, and make what I've done look like a country school just after the teacher's been licked. And I want you to be that fellow. For the present, I shall report at the office as usual, because I don't know any other place where I can get ten hours' fun a day, year in and year out.

After forty years of close acquaintance with it, I've found that work is kind to its friends and harsh to its enemies. It pays the fellow who dislikes it his exact wages, and they're generally pretty small; but it gives the man who shines up to it all the money he wants and throws in a heap of fun and satisfaction for good measure.

A broad-gauged merchant is a good deal like our friend Doc Graver, who'd cut out the washerwoman's appendix for five dollars, but would charge a thousand for showing me mine—he wants all the money that's coming to him, but he really doesn't give a cuss how much it is, just so he gets the appendix.

I've never taken any special stock in this modern theory that no fellow over forty should be given a job, or no man over sixty allowed to keep one. Of course, there's a dead-line in business, just as there is in preaching, and fifty's a good, convenient age at which to draw it; but it's been my experience that there are a lot of dead ones on both sides of it. When a man starts out to be a fool, and keeps on working steady at his trade, he usually isn't going to be any Solomon at sixty. But just because you see a lot of bald-headed sinners lined up in the front row at the show, you don't want to get humorous with every bald-headed man you meet, because the first one you tackle may be a deacon. And because a fellow has failed once or twice, or a dozen times, you don't want to set him down as a failure—unless he takes failing too easy. No man's a failure till he's dead or loses his courage, and that's the same thing. Sometimes a fellow that's been batted all over the ring for nineteen rounds lands on the solar plexus of the proposition he's tackling in the twentieth. But you can have a regiment of good business qualities, and still fail without courage, because he's the colonel, and he won't stand for any weakening at a critical time.

I learned a long while ago not to measure men with a foot-rule, and not to hire them because they were young or old, or pretty or homely, though there are certain general rules you want to keep in mind. If you were spending a million a year without making money, and you hired a young man, he'd be apt to turn in and double your expenses to make the business show a profit, and he'd be a mighty good man; but if you hired an old man, he'd probably cut your expenses to the bone and show up the money saved on the profit side; and he'd be a mighty good man, too. I hire both and then set the young man to spending and the old man to watching expenses.

Of course, the chances are that a man who hasn't got a good start at forty hasn't got it in him, but you can't run a business on the law of averages and have more than an average business. Once an old fellow who's just missed everything he's sprung at gets his hooks in, he's a tiger to stay by the meat course. And I've picked up two or three of these old man-eaters in my time who are drawing pretty large salaries with the house right now.

Whenever I hear any of this talk about carting off old fellows to the glue factory, I always think of Doc Hoover and the time they tried the "dead-line-at-fifty" racket on him, though he was something over eighty when it happened.

After I left Missouri, Doc stayed right along, year after year, in the old town, handing out hell to the sinners in public, on Sundays, and distributing corn-meal and side-meat to them on the quiet, week-days. He was a boss shepherd, you bet, and he didn't stand for any church rows or such like nonsense among his sheep. When one of them got into trouble the Doc was always on hand with his crook to pull him out, but let an old ram try to start any stampede-and-follow-the-leader-over-the-precipice foolishness, and he got the sharp end of the stick.

There was one old billy-goat in the church, a grocer named Deacon Wiggleford, who didn't really like the Elder's way of preaching. Wanted him to soak the Amalekites in his sermons, and to leave the grocery business alone. Would holler Amen! when the parson got after the money-changers in the Temple, but would shut up and look sour when he took a crack at the short-weight prune-sellers of the nineteenth century. Said he "went to church to hear the simple Gospel preached," and that may have been one of the reasons, but he didn't want it applied, because there wasn't any place where the Doc could lay it on without cutting him on the raw. The real trouble with the Deacon was that he'd never really got grace, but only a pretty fair imitation.

Well, one time after the Deacon got back from his fall trip North to buy goods, he tried to worry the Doc by telling him that all the ministers in Chicago were preaching that there wasn't any super-heated hereafter, but that each man lived through his share of hell right here on earth. Doc's face fell at first, but he cheered up mightily after nosing it over for a moment, and allowed it might be so; in fact, that he was sure it was so, as far as those fellows were concerned—they lived in Chicago. And next Sunday he preached hell so hot that the audience fairly sweat.

He wound up his sermon by deploring the tendency to atheism which he had noticed "among those merchants who had recently gone up with the caravans to Babylon for spices" (this was just his high-toned way of describing Deacon Wiggleford's trip to Chicago in a day-coach for groceries), and hoped that the goods which they had brought back were better than the theology. Of course, the old folks on the mourners' bench looked around to see how the Deacon was taking it, and the youngsters back on the gigglers' bench tittered, and everybody was happy but the Deacon. He began laying for the Doc right there. And without meaning to, it seems that I helped his little game along.

Doc Hoover used to write me every now and then, allowing that hams were scarcer in Missouri and more plentiful in my packing-house than they had any right to be, if the balance of trade was to be maintained. Said he had the demand and I had the supply, and he wanted to know what I was going to do about it. I always shipped back a tierce by fast freight, because I was afraid that if I tried to argue the point he'd come himself and take a car-load. He made a specialty of seeing that every one in town had enough food and enough religion, and he wasn't to be trifled with when he discovered a shortage of either. A mighty good salesman was lost when Doc got religion.

Well, one day something more than ten years ago he wrote in, threatening to make the usual raid on my smoke-house, and when I answered, advising him that the goods were shipped, I inclosed a little check and told him to spend it on a trip to the Holy Land which I'd seen advertised. He backed and filled over going at first, but finally the church took it out of his hands and arranged for a young fellow not long out of the Theological Seminary to fill the pulpit, and Doc put a couple of extra shirts in a grip and started off. I heard the rest of the story from Si Perkins next fall, when he brought on a couple of car-loads of steers to Chicago, and tried to stick me half a cent more than the market for them on the strength of our having come from the same town.

It seems that the young man who took Doc's place was one of these fellows with pink tea instead of red blood in his veins.

Hadn't any opinions except your opinions until he met some one else. Preached pretty, fluffy little things, and used eau de Cologne on his language. Never hit any nearer home than the unspeakable Turk, and then he was scared to death till he found out that the dark-skinned fellow under the gallery was an Armenian. (The Armenian left the church anyway, because the unspeakable Turk hadn't been soaked hard enough to suit him.) Didn't preach much from the Bible, but talked on the cussedness of Robert Elsmere and the low-downness of Trilby. Was always wanting everybody to lead the higher life, without ever really letting on what it was, or at least so any one could lay hold of it by the tail. In the end, I reckon he'd have worked around to Hoyle's games—just to call attention to their wickedness, of course.

The Pillars of the church, who'd been used to getting their religion raw from Doc Hoover, didn't take to the bottle kindly, and they all fell away except Deacon Wiggleford. He and the youngsters seemed to cotton to the new man, and just before Doc Hoover was due to get back they called a special meeting, and retired the old man with the title of pastor emeritus. They voted him two donation parties a year as long as he lived, and elected the Higher Lifer as the permanent pastor of the church. Deacon Wiggleford suggested the pastor emeritus extra. He didn't quite know what it meant, but he'd heard it in Chicago, and it sounded pretty good, and as if it ought to be a heap of satisfaction to a fellow who was being fired. Besides, it didn't cost anything, and the Deacon was one of those Christians who think that you ought to be able to save a man's immortal soul for two bits.

The Pillars were mighty hot next day when they heard what had happened, and were for calling another special meeting; but two or three of them got together and decided that it was best to lay low and avoid a row until the Doc got back.

He struck town the next week with a jugful of water from the River Jordan in one hand and a gripful of paper-weights made of wood from the Mount of Olives in the other. He was chockful of the joy of having been away and of the happiness of getting back, till they told him about the Deacon's goings on, and then he went sort of gray and old, and sat for a minute all humped up.

Si Perkins, who was one of the unregenerate, but a mighty good friend of the Doc's, was standing by, and he blurted right out: "You say the word, Doc, and we'll make the young people's society ride this rooster out of town on a rail."

"We'll make the young people's society
ride this rooster out of town on a rail"

That seemed to wake up the Elder a bit, for he shook his head and said, "No nonsense now, you Si"; and then, as he thought it over, he began to bristle and swell up; and when he stood it was to his full six feet four, and it was all man. You could see that he was boss of himself again, and when a man like old Doc Hoover is boss of himself he comes pretty near being boss of every one around him. He sent word to the Higher Lifer by one of the Pillars that he reckoned he was counting on him to preach a farewell sermon the next Sunday, and the young man, who'd been keeping in the background till whatever was going to drop, dropped, came around to welcome him in person. But while the Doc had been doing a heap of praying for grace, he didn't propose to take any chances, and he didn't see him. And he wouldn't talk to any one else, just smiled in an aggravating way, though everybody except Deacon Wiggleford and the few youngsters who'd made the trouble called to remonstrate against his paying any attention to their foolishness.

The whole town turned out the next Sunday to see the Doc step down. He sat beside the Higher Lifer on the platform, and behind them were the six deacons. When it came time to begin the services the Higher Lifer started to get up, but the Doc was already on his feet, and he whispered to him:

"Set down, young man"; and the young man sat. The Doc had a way of talking that didn't need a gun to back it up.

The old man conducted the services right through, just as he always did, except that when he'd remembered in his prayer every one in America and had worked around through Europe to Asia Minor, he lingered a trifle longer over the Turks than usual, and the list of things which he seemed to think they needed brought the Armenian back into the fold right then and there.

By the time the Doc got around to preaching, Deacon Wiggleford was looking like a fellow who'd bought a gold brick, and the Higher Lifer like the brick. Everybody else felt and looked as if they were attending the Doc's funeral, and, as usual, the only really calm and composed member of the party was the corpse.

"You will find the words of my text," Doc began, "in the revised version of the works of William Shakespeare, in the book—I mean play—of Romeo and Juliet, Act Two, Scene Two: 'Parting is such sweet sorrow that I shall say good-night till it be morrow,'" and while the audience was pulling itself together he laid out that text in four heads, each with six subheads. Began on partings, and went on a still hunt through history and religion for them. Made the audience part with Julius Caesar with regret, and had 'em sniffling at saying good-by to Napoleon and Jeff Davis. Made 'em feel that they'd lost their friends and their money, and then foreclosed the mortgage on the old homestead in a this-is-very-sad-but-I-need-the-money tone. In fact, when he had finished with Parting and was ready to begin on Sweet Sorrow, he had not only exhausted the subject, but left considerable of a deficit in it.

They say that the hour he spent on Sweet Sorrow laid over anything that the town had ever seen for sadness. Put 'em through every stage of grief from the snuffles to the snorts. Doc always was a pretty noisy preacher, but he began work on that head with soft-pedal-tremolo-stop preaching and wound up with a peroration like a steamboat explosion. Started with his illustrations dying of consumption and other peaceful diseases, and finished up with railroad wrecks. He'd been at it two hours when he got through burying the victims of his last illustration, and he was just ready to tackle his third head with six subheads. But before he took the plunge he looked at his watch and glanced up sort of surprised:

"I find," he said, "that we have consumed more time with these introductory remarks than I had intended. We would all, I know, like to say good-by till to-morrow, did our dear young brother's plans permit, but alas! he leaves us on the 2:17. Such is life; to-day we are here, to-morrow we are in St. Louis, to which our young friend must return. Usually, I don't approve of traveling on the Sabbath, but in a case like this, where the reasons are very pressing, I will lay aside my scruples, and with a committee of deacons which I have appointed see our pastor emeritus safely off."

The Doc then announced that he would preach a series of six Sunday night sermons on the six best-selling books of the month, and pronounced the benediction while the Higher Lifer and Deacon Wiggleford were trying to get the floor. But the committee of deacons had 'em by the coat-tails, and after listening to their soothing arguments the Higher Lifer decided to take the 2:17 as per schedule. When he saw the whole congregation crowding round the Doc, and the women crying over him and wanting to take him home to dinner, he understood that there'd been a mistake somewhere and that he was the mistake.

Of course the Doc never really preached on the six best-selling books. That was the first and last time he ever found a text in anything but the Bible. Si Perkins wanted to have Deacon Wiggleford before the church on charges. Said he'd been told that this pastor emeritus business was Latin, and it smelt of popery to him; but the Doc wouldn't stand for any foolishness. Allowed that the special meeting was illegal, and that settled it; and he reckoned they could leave the Deacon's case to the Lord. But just the same, the small boys used to worry Wiggleford considerably by going into his store and yelling: "Mother says she doesn't want any more of those pastor emeritus eggs," or, "She'll send it back if you give us any more of that dead-line butter."

If the Doc had laid down that Sunday, there'd probably have been a whole lot of talk and tears over his leaving, but in the end, the Higher Lifer or some other fellow would have had his job, and he'd have become one of those nice old men for whom every one has a lot of respect but no special use. But he kept right on, owning his pulpit and preaching in it, until the Great Call was extended to him.

I'm a good deal like the Doc—willing to preach a farewell sermon whenever it seems really necessary, but some other fellow's.

Your affectionate father,

JOHN GRAHAM.

II.

From John Graham, at the Schweitzerkasenhof, Carlsbad, to his son, Pierrepont, at the Union Stock Yards, Chicago.

The head of the lard department has died suddenly, and Pierrepont has suggested to the old man that there is a silver lining to that cloud of sorrow.

CARLSBAD, October 20, 189-.

Dear Pierrepont: I've cabled the house that you will manage the lard department, or try to, until I get back; but beyond that I can't see. Four weeks doesn't give you much time to prove that you are the best man in the shop for the place, but it gives you enough to prove that you ain't. You've got plenty of rope. If you know how to use it you can throw your steer and brand it; if you don't, I suppose I won't find much more than a grease-spot where the lard department was, when I get back to the office. I'm hopeful, but I'm a good deal like the old deacon back in Missouri who thought that games of chance were sinful, and so only bet on sure things—and I'm not betting.

Naturally, when a young fellow steps up into a big position, it breeds jealousy among those whom he's left behind and uneasiness among those to whom he's pulled himself up. Between them he's likely to be subjected to a lot of petty annoyances. But he's in the fix of a dog with fleas who's chasing a rabbit—if he stops to snap at the tickling on his tail, he's going to lose his game dinner.

Even as temporary head of the lard department you're something of a pup, and where there's dog there's fleas. You've simply got to get used to them, and have sense enough to know that they're not eating you up when they're only nibbling a little at your hide. And you don't want to let any one see that a flea-bite can worry you, either. A pup that's squirming and wriggling and nosing around the seat of the trouble whenever one of his little friends gets busy, is kicked out into the cold, sad night in the end. But a wise dog lies before the fire with a droop in his ear and a dreamy look in his eyes until it gets to the point where he can't stand 'em any longer. Then he sneaks off under the dining-room table and rolls them out into the carpet.

There are two breeds of little things in business—those that you can't afford to miss and those that you can't afford to notice. The first are the details of your own work and those of the men under you. The second are the little tricks and traps that the envious set around you. A trick is always so low that a high-stepper can walk right over it.

When a fellow comes from the outside to an important position with a house he generally gets a breathing-space while the old men spar around taking his measure and seeing if he sizes up to his job. They give him the benefit of the doubt, and if he shows up strong and shifty on his feet they're apt to let him alone. But there isn't any doubt in your case; everybody's got you sized up, or thinks he has, and those who've been over you will find it hard to accept you as an equal, and those who've been your equals will be slow to regard you as a superior. When you've been Bill to a man, it comes awkward for him to call you mister. He may do it to your face, but you're always Bill again when you've turned the corner.

Of course, everybody's going to say you're an accident. Prove it. Show that you're a regular head-on collision when anything gets in your way. They're going to say that you've got a pull. Prove it—by taking up all the slack that they give you. Back away from controversy, but stand up stubborn as a mule to the fellow who's hunting trouble. I believe in ruling by love, all right, but it's been my experience that there are a lot of people in the world whom you've got to make understand that you're ready to heave a brick if they don't come when you call them. These men mistake kindness for weakness and courtesy for cowardice. Of course, it's the exception when a fellow of this breed can really hurt you, but the exception is the thing that you always want to keep your eye skinned for in business. When it's good growing weather and the average of the crop is ninety-five, you should remember that old Satan may be down in Arizona cooking up a sizzler for the cornbelt; or that off Cuba-ways, where things get excited easy, something special in the line of tornadoes may be ghost-dancing and making ready to come North to bust you into bits, if it catches you too far away from the cyclone cellar. When a boy's face shines with soap, look behind his ears.

Up to this point you've been seeing business from the seat of the man who takes orders; now you're going to find out what sort of a snap the fellow who gives them has. You're not even exchanging one set of worries for another, because a good boss has to carry all his own and to share those of his men. He must see without spying; he must hear without sneaking; he must know without asking. It takes a pretty good guesser to be a boss.

The first banana-skin which a lot of fellows step on when they're put over other men is a desire to be too popular. Of course, it's a nice thing to have everyone stand up and cheer when your name is mentioned, but it's mighty seldom that that happens to any one till he's dead. You can buy a certain sort of popularity anywhere with soft soap and favors; but you can't buy respect with anything but justice, and that's the only popularity worth having.

You'll find that this world is so small, and that most men in it think they're so big, that you can't step out in any direction without treading on somebody's corns, but unless you keep moving, the fellow who's in a hurry to get somewhere is going to fetch up on your bunion. Some men are going to dislike you because you're smooth, and others because you have a brutal way of telling the truth. You're going to repel some because they think you're cold, and others will cross the street when they see you coming because they think you slop over. One fellow won't like you because you're got curly hair, and another will size you up as a stiff because you're bald. Whatever line of conduct you adopt you're bound to make some enemies, but so long as there's a choice I want you to make yours by being straightforward and just. You'll have the satisfaction of knowing that every enemy you make by doing the square thing is a rascal at heart. Don't fear too much the enemy you make by saying No, nor trust too much the friend you make by saying Yes.

Speaking of being popular naturally calls to mind the case of a fellow from the North named Binder, who moved to our town when I was a boy, and allowed that he was going into the undertaking business. Absalom Magoffin, who had had all the post-mortem trade of the town for forty years, was a queer old cuss, and he had some mighty aggravating ways. Never wanted to talk anything but business. Would buttonhole you on the street, and allow that, while he wasn't a doctor, he had had to cover up a good many of the doctor's mistakes in his time, and he didn't just like your symptoms. Said your looks reminded him of Bill Shorter, who' went off sudden in the fifties, and was buried by the Masons with a brass band. Asked if you remembered Bill, and that peculiar pasty look about his skin. Naturally, this sort of thing didn't make Ab any too popular, and so Binder got a pretty warm welcome when he struck town.

He started right out by saying that he didn't see any good reason why an undertaker should act as if he was the next of kin. Was always stopping people on the streets to tell them the latest, and yelling out the point in a horse-laugh. Everybody allowed that jolly old Binder had the right idea; and that Magoffin might as well shut up shop. Every one in town wanted to see him officiate at a funeral, and there was a lot of talk about encouraging new enterprises, but it didn't come to anything. No one appeared to have any public spirit.

Seemed as if we'd never had a healthier spring than that one.

Couldn't fetch a nigger, even. The most unpopular man in town, Miser Dosher, came down with pneumonia in December, and every one went around saying how sad it was that there was no hope, and watching for Binder to start for the house. But in the end Dosher rallied and "went back on the town," as Si Perkins put it. Then the Hoskins-Bustard crowds took a crack at each other one court day, but it was mighty poor shooting. Ham Hoskins did get a few buckshot in his leg, and that had to come off, but there were no complications.

By this time Binder, though he still laughed and cracked his jokes, was beginning to get sort of discouraged. But Si Perkins used to go round and cheer him up by telling him that it was bound to come his way in the end, and that when it did come it would come with a rush.

Then, all of a sudden, something happened—yellow jack dropped in from down New Orleans way, and half the people in town had it inside a week and the other half were so blamed scared that they thought they had it. But through it all Binder never once lost his merry, cheery ways. Luckily it was a mild attack and everybody got well; but it made it mighty easy for Doc Hoover to bring sinners tinder conviction for a year to come.

When it was all over Binder didn't have a friend in town. Leaked out little by little that as soon as one of the men who'd been cheering for jolly old Binder got yellow jack, the first thing he did was to make his wife swear that she'd have Magoffin do the planting.

You see, that while a man may think it's all foolishness for an undertaker to go around solemn and sniffling, he'll be a little slow about hiring a fellow to officiate at his funeral who's apt to take a sense of humor to it.

Si Perkins was the last one to get well, and the first time he was able to walk as far as the store he made a little speech. Wanted to know if we were going to let a Connecticut Yankee trifle with our holiest emotions. Thought he ought to be given a chance to crack his blanked New England jokes in Hades. Allowed that the big locust in front of Binder's store made an ideal spot for a jolly little funeral. Of course Si wasn't exactly consistent in this, but, as he used to say, it's the consistent men who keep the devil busy, because no one's ever really consistent except in his cussedness. It's been my experience that consistency is simply a steel hoop around a small mind—it keeps it from expanding.

Well, Si hadn't more than finished before the whole crowd was off whooping down the street toward Binder's. As soon as they got in range of the house they began shooting at the windows and yelling for him to come out if he was a man, but it appeared that Binder wasn't a man—leastways, he didn't come out—and investigation showed that he was streaking it back for Connecticut.

I simply mention this little incident as an example of the fact that popularity is a mighty uncertain critter and a mighty unsafe one to hitch your wagon to. It'll eat all the oats you bring it, and then kick you as you're going out of the stall. It's happened pretty often in my time that I've seen a crowd pelt a man with mud, go away, and, returning a few months or a few years later, and finding him still in the same place, throw bouquets at him. But that, mark you, was because first and last he was standing in the right place.

It's been my experience that there are more cases of hate at first sight than of love at first sight, and that neither of them is of any special consequence. You tend strictly to your job of treating your men square, without slopping over, and when you get into trouble there'll be a little bunch to line up around you with their horns down to keep the wolves from cutting you out of the herd.

Your affectionate father,

JOHN GRAHAM.

III.

_____

From John Graham, at the Schweitzerkasenhof, Carlsbad, to his son, Pierrepont, at the Union Stock Yards, Chicago.

A friend of the young man has just presented a letter of introduction to the old man, and has exchanged a large bunch of stories for a small roll of bills.

CARLSBAD, October 24, 189-.

Dear Pierrepont: Yesterday your old college friend, Clarence, blew in from Monte Carlo, where he had been spending a few days in the interests of science, and presented your letter of introduction. Said he still couldn't understand just how it happened, because he had figured it out by logarithms and trigonometry and differential calculus and a lot of other high-priced studies that he'd taken away from Harvard, and that it was a cinch on paper. Was so sure that he could have proved his theory right if he'd only had a little more money that it hardly seemed worth while to tell him that the only thing he could really prove with his system was old Professor Darwin's theory that men and monkeys began life in the same cage. It never struck me before, but I'll bet the Professor got that idea while he was talking with some of his students.

Personally, I don't know a great deal about gambling, because all I ever spent for information on the subject was $2.75—my fool horse broke in the stretch—and that was forty years ago; but first and last I've heard a lot of men explain how it happened that they hadn't made a hog-killing. Of course, there must be a winning end to gambling, but all that these men have been able to tell about is the losing end. And I gather from their experiences that when a fellow does a little gambling on the side, it's usually on the wrong side.

The fact of the matter is, that the race-horse, the faro tiger, and the poker kitty have bigger appetites than any healthy critter has a right to have; and after you've fed a tapeworm, there's mighty little left for you. Following the horses may be pleasant exercise at the start, but they're apt to lead you to the door of the poorhouse or the jail at the finish.

To get back to Clarence; he took about an hour to dock his cargo of hard luck, and another to tell me how strange it was that there was no draft from his London bankers waiting to welcome him. Naturally, I haven't lived for sixty years among a lot of fellows who've been trying to drive a cold-chisel between me and my bank account, without being able to smell a touch coming a long time before it overtakes me, and Clarence's intentions permeated his cheery conversation about as thoroughly as a fertilizer factory does a warm summer night. Of course, he gave me every opportunity to prove that I was a gentleman and to suggest delicately that I should be glad if he would let me act as his banker in this sudden emergency, but as I didn't show any signs of being a gentleman and a banker, he was finally forced to come out and ask me in coarse commercial words to lend him a hundred. Said it hurt him to have to do it on such short acquaintance, but I couldn't see that he was suffering any real pain.

Frankly, I shouldn't have lent Clarence a dollar on his looks or his story, for they both struck me as doubtful collateral, but so long as he had a letter from you, asking me to "do anything in my power to oblige him, or to make his stay in Carlsbad pleasant," I let him have the money on your account, to which I have written the cashier to charge it. Of course, I hope Clarence will pay you back, but I think you will save bookkeeping by charging it off to experience. I've usually found that these quick, glad borrowers are slow, sad payers. And when a fellow tells you that it hurts him to have to borrow, you can bet that the thought of having to pay is going to tie him up into a bow-knot of pain.

Right here I want to caution you against giving away your signature to every Clarence and Willie that happens along. When your name is on a note it stands only for money, but when it's on a letter of introduction or recommendation it stands for your judgment of ability and character, and you can't call it in at the end of thirty days, either. Giving a letter of introduction is simply lending your name with a man as collateral, and if he's no good you can't have the satisfaction of redeeming your indorsement, even; and you're discredited. The first thing that a young merchant must learn is that his brand must never appear on a note, or a ham, or a man that isn't good. I reckon that the devil invented the habit of indorsing notes and giving letters to catch the fellows he couldn't reach with whisky and gambling.

Of course, letters of introduction have their proper use, but about nine out of ten of them are simply a license to some Clarence to waste an hour of your time and to graft on you for the luncheon and cigars. It's getting so that a fellow who's almost a stranger to me doesn't think anything of asking for a letter of introduction to one who's a total stranger. You can't explain to these men, because when you try to let them down easy by telling them that you haven't had any real opportunity to know what their special abilities are, they always come back with an, "Oh! that's all right—just say a word and refer to anything you like about me."

I give them the letter then, unsealed, and though, of course, they're not supposed to read it, I have reason to think that they do, because I've never heard of one of those letters being presented. I use the same form on all of them, and after they've pumped their thanks into me and rushed around the corner, they find in the envelope: "This will introduce Mr. Gallister. While I haven't had the pleasure of any extended acquaintance with Mr. Gallister, I like his nerve."

It's a mighty curious thing, but a lot of men who have no claim on you, and who wouldn't think of asking for money, will panhandle both sides of a street for favors that mean more than money. Of course, it's the easy thing and the pleasant thing not to refuse, and after all, most men think, it doesn't cost anything but a few strokes of the pen, and so they will give a fellow that they wouldn't ordinarily play on their friends as a practical joke, a nice sloppy letter of introduction to them; or hand out to a man that they wouldn't give away as a booby prize, a letter of recommendation in which they crack him up as having all the qualities necessary for an A1 Sunday-school superintendent and bank president.

Now that you are a boss you will find that every other man who comes to your desk is going to ask you for something; in fact, the difference between being a sub and a boss is largely a matter of asking for things and of being asked for things. But it's just as one of those poets said—you can't afford to burn down the glue factory to stimulate the demand for glue stock, or words to that effect.

Of course, I don't mean by this that I want you to be one of those fellows who swell out like a ready-made shirt and brag that they "never borrow and never lend." They always think that this shows that they are sound, conservative business men, but, as a matter of fact, it simply stamps them as mighty mean little cusses. It's very superior, I know, to say that you never borrow, but most men have to at one time or another, and then they find that the never-borrow-never-lend platform is a mighty inconvenient one to be standing on. Be just in business and generous out of it. A fellow's generosity needs a heap of exercise to keep it in good condition, and the hand that writes out checks gets cramped easier than the hand that takes them in. You want to keep them both limber.

While I don't believe in giving with a string tied to every dollar, or doing up a gift in so many conditions that the present is lost in the wrappings, it's a good idea not to let most people feel that money can be had for the asking. If you do, they're apt to go into the asking business for a living. But these millionaires who give away a hundred thousand or so, with the understanding that the other fellow will raise another hundred thousand or so, always remind me of a lot of boys coaxing a dog into their yard with a hunk of meat, so that they can tie a tin can to his tail—the pup edges up licking his chops at the thought of the provisions and hanging his tail at the thought of the hardware. If he gets the meat, he's got to run himself to death to get rid of the can.

While we're on this subject of favors I want to impress on you the importance of deciding promptly. The man who can make up his mind quick, makes up other people's minds for them. Decision is a sharp knife that cuts clear and straight and lays bare the fat and the lean; indecision, a dull one that hacks and tears and leaves ragged edges behind it. Say yes or no—seldom perhaps. Some people have such fertile imaginations that they will take a grain of hope and grow a large definite promise with bark on it overnight, and later, when you come to pull that out of their brains by the roots, it hurts, and they holler.

When a fellow asks for a job in your department there may be reasons why you hate to give him a clear-cut refusal, but tell him frankly that you see no possibility of placing him, and while he may not like the taste of the medicine, he swallows it and it's down and forgotten. But you say to him that you're very sorry your department is full just now, but that you think a place will come along later and that he shall have the first call on it, and he goes away with his teeth in a job. You've simply postponed your trouble for a few weeks or months. And trouble postponed always has to be met with accrued interest.

Never string a man along in business. It isn't honest and it isn't good policy. Either's a good reason, but taken together they head the list of good reasons.

Of course, I don't mean that you want to go rampaging along, trampling on people's feelings and goring every one who sticks up a head in your path. But there's no use shilly-shallying and doddering with people who ask questions and favors they have no right to ask. Don't hurt any one if you can help it, but if you must, a clean, quick wound heals soonest.

When you can, it's better to refuse a request by letter. In a letter you need say only what you choose; in a talk you may have to say more than you want to say.

With the best system in the world you'll find it impossible, however, to keep a good many people who have no real business with you from seeing you and wasting your time, because a broad-gauged merchant must be accessible. When a man's office is policed and every one who sees him has to prove that he's taken the third degree and is able to give the grand hailing sign, he's going to miss a whole lot of things that it would be mighty valuable for him to know. Of course, the man whose errand could be attended to by the office-boy is always the one who calls loudest for the boss, but with a little tact you can weed out most of these fellows, and it's better to see ten bores than to miss one buyer. A house never gets so big that it can afford to sniff at a hundred-pound sausage order, or to feel that any customer is so small that it can afford not to bother with him. You've got to open a good many oysters to find a pearl.

You should answer letters just as you answer men—promptly, courteously, and decisively. Of course, you don't ever want to go off half-cocked and bring down a cow instead of the buck you're aiming at, but always remember that game is shy and that you can't shoot too quick after you've once got it covered. When I go into a fellow's office and see his desk buried in letters with the dust on them, I know that there are cobwebs in his head. Foresight is the quality that makes a great merchant, but a man who has his desk littered with yesterday's business has no time to plan for to-morrow's.

The only letters that can wait are those which provoke a hot answer. A good hot letter is always foolish, and you should never write a foolish thing if you can say it to the man instead, and never say it if you can forget it. The wisest man may make an ass of himself to-day, over to-day's provocation, but he won't tomorrow. Before being used, warm words should be run into the cooling-room until the animal heat is out of them. Of course, there's no use in a fool's waiting, because there's no room in a small head in which to lose a grievance.

Speaking of small heads naturally calls to mind a gold brick named Solomon Saunders that I bought when I was a good deal younger and hadn't been buncoed so often. I got him with a letter recommending him as a sort of happy combination of the three wise men of the East and the nine muses, and I got rid of him with one in which I allowed that he was the whole dozen.

I really hired Sol because he reminded me of some one I'd known and liked, though I couldn't just remember at the time who it was; but one day, after he'd been with me about a week, it came to me in a flash that he was the living image of old Bucker, a billy-goat I'd set aheap of store by when I was a boy. That was a lesson to me on the foolishness of getting sentimental in business. I never think of the old homestead that echo doesn't answer, "Give up!"; or hear from it without getting a bill for having been born there.

Sol had started out in life to be a great musician. Had raised the hair for the job and had kept his finger-nails cut just right for it, but somehow, when he played "My Old Kentucky Home," nobody sobbed softly in the fourth row. You see, he could play a piece absolutely right and meet every note just when it came due, but when he got through it was all wrong. That was Sol in business, too. He knew just the right rule for doing everything and did it just that way, and yet everything he did turned out to be a mistake. Made it twice as aggravating because you couldn't consistently find fault with him. If you'd given Sol the job of making over the earth he'd have built it out of the latest text-book on "How to Make the World Better," and have turned out something as correct as a spike-tail coat—and every one would have wanted to die to get out of it.

Then, too, I never saw such a cuss for system. Other men

would forget costs and prices, but Sol never did. Seemed he ran his memory by system. Had a way when there was a change in the price-list of taking it home and setting it to poetry. Used "Ring Out, Wild Bells," by A. Tennyson, for a bull market—remember he began it "Ring Off, Wild Bulls"—and "Break, Break, Break," for a bear one.

It used to annoy me considerable when I asked him the price of pork tenderloins to have him mumble through two or three verses till he fetched it up, but I didn't have any real kick coming till he got ambitious and I had to wait till he'd hummed half through a grand opera to get a quotation on pickled pigs' feet in kits. I felt that we had reached the parting of the ways then, but I didn't like to point out his way too abruptly, because the friend who had unloaded him on us was pretty important to me in my business just then, and he seemed to be all wrapped up in Sol's making a hit with us.

It's been my experience, though, that sometimes when you can't kick a man out of the back door without a row, you can get him to walk out the front way voluntarily. So when I get stuck with a fellow that, for some reason, it isn't desirable to fire, I generally promote him and raise his pay. Some of these weak sisters I make the assistant boss of the machine-shop and some of the bone-meal mill. I didn't dare send Sol to the machine-shop, because I knew he wouldn't have been there a week before he'd have had the shop running on Götterdämmerung or one of those other cuss-word operas of Wagner's. But the strong point of a bone-meal mill is bone-dust, and the strong point of bone-dust is smell, and the strong point of its smell is its staying qualities. Naturally it's the sort of job for which you want a bald-headed man, because a fellow who's got nice thick curls will cheat the house by taking a good deal of the product home with him. To tell the truth, Sol's hair had been worrying me almost as much as his system. When I hired him I'd supposed he'd finally molt it along with his musical tail-feathers. I had a little talk with him then, in which I hinted at the value of looking clear-cut and trim and of giving sixteen ounces to the pound, but the only result of it was that he went off and bought a pot of scented vaseline and grew another inch of hair for good measure. It seemed a pity now, so long as I was after his scalp, not to get it with the hair on.

Sol had never seen a bone-meal mill, but it flattered him mightily to be promoted into the manufacturing end, "where a fellow could get ahead faster," and he said good-by to the boys in the office with his nose in the air, where he kept it, I reckon, during the rest of his connection with the house.

If Sol had stuck it out for a month at the mill I'd have known that he had the right stuff in him somewhere and have taken him back into the office after a good rub-down with pumice-stone. But he turned up the second day, smelling of violet soap and bone-meal, and he didn't sing his list of grievances, either. Started right in by telling me how, when he got into a street-car, all the other passengers sort of faded out; and how his landlady insisted on serving his meals in his room. Almost foamed at the mouth when I said the office seemed a little close and opened the window, and he quoted some poetry about that being "the most unkindest cut of all." Wound up by wanting to know how he was going to get it out of his hair.

I broke it to him as gently as I could that it would have to wear out or be cut out, and tried to make him see that it was better to be a bald-headed boss on a large salary than a curly-headed clerk on a small one; but, in the end, he resigned, taking along a letter from me to the friend who had recommended him and some of my good bone-meal.

I didn't grudge him the fertilizer, but I did feel sore that he hadn't left me a lock of his hair, till some one saw him a few days later, dodging along with his collar turned up and his hat pulled down, looking like a new-clipped lamb. I heard, too, that the fellow who had given him the wise-men-muses letter to me was so impressed with the almost exact duplicate of it which I gave Sol, and with the fact that I had promoted him so soon, that he concluded he must have let a good man get by him, and hired him himself.

Sol was a failure as a musician because, while he knew all the notes, he had nothing in himself to add to them when he played them. It's easy to learn all the notes that make good music and all the rules that make good business, but a fellow's got to add the fine curves to them himself if he wants to do anything more than beat the bass-drum all his life. Some men think that rules should be made of cast iron; I believe that they should be made of rubber, so that they can be stretched to fit any particular case and then spring back into shape again. The really important part of a rule is the exception to it.

Your affectionate father,

JOHN GRAHAM.

P.S.—Leave for home to-morrow.

IV.

From John Graham, at the Hotel Cecil, London, to his son, Pierrepont, at the Union Stock Yards, Chicago.

The old man has just finished going through the young man's first report as manager of the lard department, and he finds it suspiciously good.

LONDON, December 1, 189-.

Dear Pierrepont: Your first report; looks so good that I'm a little afraid of it. Figures don't lie, I know, but that's, only because they can't talk. As a matter of fact, they're just as truthful as the man who's behind them.

It's been my experience that there are two kinds of figures—educated and uneducated ones—and that the first are a good deal like the people who have had the advantage of a college education on the inside and the disadvantage of a society finish on the outside—they're apt to tell you only the smooth and the pleasant things. Of course, it's mighty nice to be told that the shine of your shirt-front is blinding the floor-manager's best girl; but if there's a hole in the seat of your pants you ought to know that, too, because sooner or later you've got to turn your back to the audience.

Now don't go off half-cocked and think I'm allowing that you ain't truthful; because I think you are—reasonably so—and I'm sure that everything you say in your report is true. But is there anything you don't say in it?

A good many men are truthful on the installment plan—that

37

is, they tell their boss all the good things in sight about their end of the business and then dribble out the bad ones like a fellow who's giving you a list of his debts. They'll yell for a week that the business of their department has increased ten per cent., and then own up in a whisper that their selling cost has increased twenty. In the end, that always creates a worse impression than if both sides of the story had been told at once or the bad had been told first. It's like buying a barrel of apples that's been deaconed—after you've found that the deeper you go the meaner and wormier the fruit, you forget all about the layer of big, rosy, wax-finished pippins which was on top.

I never worry about the side of a proposition that I can see; what I want to get a look at is the side that's out of sight. The bugs always snuggle down on the under side of the stone.

The best year we ever had—in our minds—was one when the superintendent of the packing-house wanted an increase in his salary, and, to make a big showing, swelled up his inventory like a poisoned pup. It took us three months, to wake up to what had happened, and a year to get over feeling as if there was sand in our eyes when we compared the second showing with the first. An optimist is as bad as a drunkard when he comes to figure up results in business—he sees double. I employ optimists to get results and pessimists to figure them up.

After I've charged off in my inventory for wear and tear and depreciation, I deduct a little more just for luck—bad luck. That's the only sort of luck a merchant can afford to make a part of his calculations.

The fellow who said you can't make a silk purse out of a sow's ear wasn't on to the packing business. You can make the purse and you can fill it, too, from the same critter. What you can't do is to load up a report with moonshine or an inventory with wind, and get anything more substantial than a moonlight sail toward bankruptcy. The kittens of a wildcat are wildcats, and there's no use counting on their being angoras.

Speaking of educated pigs naturally calls to mind Jake

Solzenheimer and the lard that he sold half a cent a pound cheaper than any one else in the business could make it. That was a long time ago, when the packing business was still on the bottle, and when the hogs that came to Chicago got only a common-school education and graduated as plain hams and sides and lard and sausage. Literature hadn't hit the hog business then. It was just Graham's hams or Smith's lard, and there were no poetical brands or high-art labels.

Well, sir, one day I heard that this Jake was offering lard to the trade at half a cent under the market, and that he'd had the nerve to label it "Driven Snow Leaf." Told me, when I ran up against him on the street, that he'd got the name from a song which began, "Once I was pure as the driven snow." Said it made him feel all choky and as if he wanted to be a better man, so he'd set out to make the song famous in the hope of its helping others. Allowed that this was a hard world, and that it was little enough we could do in our business life to scatter sunshine along the way; but he proposed that every can which left his packing-house after this should carry the call to a better life into some humble home.

I let him lug that sort of stuff to the trough till he got tired, and then I looked him square in the eye and went right at him with:

"Jake, what you been putting in that lard?" because I knew mighty well that there was something in it which had never walked on four feet and fattened up on fifty-cent corn and then paid railroad fare from the Missouri River to Chicago. There are a good many things I don't know, but hogs ain't one of them.

Jake just grinned at me and swore that there was nothing in his lard except the pure juice of the hog; so I quit fooling with him and took a can of "Driven Snow" around to our chemist. It looked like lard and smelt like lard—in fact, it looked better than real lard: too white and crinkly and tempting on top. And the next day the chemist came down to my office and told me that "Driven Snow" must have been driven through a candle factory, because it had picked up about twenty per cent. of paraffin wax somewhere.

Of course, I saw now why Jake was able to undersell us all, but it was mighty important to knock out "Driven Snow" with the trade in just the right way, because most of our best customers had loaded up with it. So I got the exact formula from the chemist and had about a hundred sample cans made up, labeling each one "Wandering Boy Leaf Lard," and printing on the labels: "This lard contains twenty per cent. of paraffin."

I sent most of these cans, with letters of instruction, to our men through the country. Then I waited until it was Jake's time to be at the Live Stock Exchange, and happened in with a can of "Wandering Boy" under my arm. It didn't take me long to get into conversation with Jake, and as we talked I swung that can around until it attracted his attention, and he up and asked:

"What you got there, Graham?"

"Oh, that," I answered, slipping the can behind my back— "that's a new lard we're putting out—something not quite so expensive as our regular brand."

Jake stopped grinning then and gave me a mighty sharp look.

"Lemme have a squint at it," says he, trying not to show too keen an interest in his face.

I held back a little; then I said: "Well, I don't just know as I ought to show you this. We haven't regularly put it on the market, and this can ain't a fair sample of what we can do; but so long as I sort of got the idea from you I might as well tell you. I'd been thinking over what you said about that lard of yours, and while they were taking a collection in church the other day the soprano up and sings a mighty touching song. It began, 'Where is my wandering boy to-night?' and by the time she was through I was feeling so mushy and sobby that I put a five instead of a one into the plate by mistake. I've been thinking ever since that the attention of the country ought to be called to that song, and so I've got up this missionary lard"; and I shoved the can of "Wandering Boy" under his eyes, giving him time to read the whole label.

"H—l!" he said.

"Yes," I answered; "that's it. Good lard gone wrong; but it's going to do a great work."

Jake's face looked like the Lost Tribes—the whole bunch of 'em—as the thing soaked in; and then he ran his arm through mine and drew me off into a corner.

"That's it—good lard gone wrong"

"Graham," said he, "let's drop this cussed foolishness. You keep dark about this and we'll divide the lard trade of the country."

I pretended not to understand what he was driving at, but reached out and grasped his hand and wrung it. "Yes, yes, Jake,"

I said; "we'll stand shoulder to shoulder and make the lard business one grand sweet song," and then I choked him off by calling another fellow into the conversation. It hardly seemed worth while to waste time telling Jake what he was going to find out when he got back to his office—that there wasn't any lard business to divide, because I had hogged it all.

You see, my salesmen had taken their samples of "Wandering Boy" around to the buyers and explained that it was made from the same formula as "Driven Snow," and could be bought at the same price. They didn't sell any "Boy," of course—that wasn't the idea; but they loaded up the trade with our regular brand, to take the place of the "Driven Snow," which was shipped back to Jake by the car-lot.

Since then, when anything looks too snowy and smooth and good at the first glance, I generally analyze it for paraffin. I've found that this is a mighty big world for a square man and a mighty small world for a crooked one.

I simply mention these things in a general way. I've confidence that you're going to make good as head of the lard department, and if, when I get home, I find that your work analyzes seventy-five per cent, as pure as your report I shall be satisfied. In the meanwhile I shall instruct the cashier to let you draw a hundred dollars a week, just to show that I haven't got a case of faith without works. I reckon the extra twenty-five per will come in mighty handy now that you're within a month of marrying Helen.

I'm still learning how to treat an old wife, and so I can't give you many pointers about a young one. For while I've been married as long as I've been in business, and while I know all the curves of the great American hog, your ma's likely to spring a new one on me tomorrow. No man really knows anything about women except a widower, and he forgets it when he gets ready to marry again. And no woman really knows anything about men except a widow, and she's got to forget it before she's willing to marry again. The one thing you can know is that, as a general proposition, a woman is a little better than the man for whom she cares. For when a woman's bad, there's always a man at the bottom of it; and when a man's good, there's always a woman at the bottom of that, too.

The fact of the matter is, that while marriages may be made in heaven, a lot of them are lived in hell and end in South Dakota. But when a man has picked out a good woman he holds four hearts, and he needn't be afraid to draw cards if he's got good nerve. If he hasn't, he's got no business to be sitting in games of chance. The best woman in the world will begin trying out a man before she's been married to him twenty-four hours; and unless he can smile over the top of a four-flush and raise the ante, she's going to rake in the breeches and keep them.

The great thing is to begin right. Marriage is a close corporation, and unless a fellow gets the controlling interest at the start he can't pick it up later. The partner who owns fifty-one per cent. of the stock in any business is the boss, even if the other is allowed to call himself president. There's only two jobs for a man in his own house—one's boss and the other's office-boy, and a fellow naturally falls into the one for which he's fitted.

Of course, when I speak of a fellow's being boss in his own home, I simply mean that, in a broad way, he's going to shape the policy of the concern. When a man goes sticking his nose into the running of the house, he's apt to get it tweaked, and while he's busy drawing *it* back out of danger he's going to get his leg pulled, too. You let your wife tend to the housekeeping and you focus on earning money with which she can keep house. Of course, in one way, it's mighty nice of a man to help around the place, but it's been my experience that the fellows who tend to all the small jobs at home never get anything else to tend to at the office. In the end, it's usually cheaper to give all your attention to your business and to hire a plumber.

You don't want to get it into your head, though, that because your wife hasn't any office-hours she has a soft thing. A lot of men go around sticking out their chests and wondering why their wives have so much trouble with the help, when they are able to handle their clerks so easy. If you really want to know, you lift two of your men out of their revolving-chairs, and hang one over a forty-horse-power cook-stove that's booming along under forced draft so that your dinner won't be late, with a turkey that's gobbling for basting in one oven, and a cake that's gone back on you in a low, underhand way in another, and sixteen different things boiling over on top and mixing up their smells. And you set the other at a twelve-hour stunt of making all the beds you've mussed, and washing all the dishes you've used, and cleaning all the dust you've kicked up, and you boss the whole while the baby yells with colic over your arm—you just try this with two of your men and see how long it is before there's rough-house on the Wabash. Yet a lot of fellows come home after their wives have had a day of this and blow around about how tired and overworked they are, and wonder why home isn't happier. Don't you ever forget that it's a blamed sight easier to keep cool in front of an electric fan than a cook-stove, and that you can't subject the best temper in the world to 500 degrees Fahrenheit without warming it up a bit. And don't you add to your wife's troubles by saying how much better you could do it, but stand pat and thank the Lord you've got a snap.

I remember when old Doc Hoover, just after his wife died, bought a mighty competent nigger, Aunt Tempy, to cook and look after the house for him. She was the boss cook, you bet, and she could fry a chicken into a bird of paradise just as easy as the Doc could sizzle a sinner into a pretty tolerable Christian.

The old man took his religion with the bristles on, and he wouldn't stand for any Sunday work in his house. Told Tempy to cook enough for two days on Saturday and to serve three cold meals on Sunday.

Tempy sniffed a little, but she'd been raised well and didn't talk back. That first Sunday Doc got his cold breakfast all right, but before he'd fairly laid into it Tempy trotted out a cup of hot coffee. That made the old man rage at first, but finally he allowed that, seeing it was made, there was no special harm in taking a sup or two, but not to let it occur again. A few minutes later he called back to Tempy in the kitchen and asked her if she'd been sinful enough to make two cups.

Doc's dinner was ready for him when he got back from church, and it was real food—that is to say, hot food, a-sizzling and a-smoking from the stove. Tempy told around afterward that the way the old man went for her about it made her feel mighty proud and set-up over her new master. But she just stood there dripping perspiration and good nature until the Doc had wound up by allowing that there was only one part of the hereafter where meals were cooked on Sunday, and that she'd surely get a mention on the bill of fare there as dark meat, well done, if she didn't repent, and then she blurted out:

"Law, chile, you go 'long and 'tend to yo' preaching and I'll 'tend to my cookin'; yo' can't fight the debbil with snow-balls." And what's more, the Doc didn't, not while Aunt Tempy was living.

There isn't any moral to this, but there's a hint in it to mind your own business at home as well as at the office. I sail to-morrow. I'm feeling in mighty good spirits, and I hope I'm not going to find anything at your end of the line to give me a relapse.

Your affectionate father,

JOHN GRAHAM.

V.

From John Graham, at the Waldorf-Astoria, New York, to his son, Pierrepont, at the Union Stock Yards, Chicago.

The young man has hinted vaguely of a quarrel between himself and Helen Heath, who is in New York with her mother, and has suggested that the old man act as peacemaker.

NEW YORK, December 8, 189-.

Dear Pierrepont: I've been afraid all along that you were going to spoil the only really sensible thing you've ever done by making some fool break, so as soon as I got your letter I started right out to trail down Helen and her ma. I found them hived up here in the hotel, and Miss Helen was so sweet to your poor old pa that I saw right off she had a stick cut for his son. Of course, I didn't let on that I knew anything about a quarrel, but I gradually steered the conversation around to you, and while I don't want to hurt your feelings, I am violating no confidence when I tell you that the mention of your name aroused about the same sort of enthusiasm that Bill Bryan's does in Wall Street—only Helen is a lady and so she couldn't cuss. But it wasn't the language of flowers that I saw in her eyes. So I told her that she must make allowances for you, as you were only a half-baked boy, and that, naturally, if she stuck a hat-pin into your crust she was going to strike a raw streak here and there.

She sat up a little at that, and started in to tell me that while you had said "some very, very cruel, cruel things to her, still—"

But I cut her short by allowing that, sorry as I was to own it, I was afraid you had a streak of the brute in you, and I only hoped that you wouldn't take it out on her after you were married.

Well, sir, the way she flared up, I thought that all the Fourth of July fireworks had gone off at once. The air was full of trouble—trouble in set pieces and bombs and sizzy rockets and sixteen-ball Roman candles, and all pointed right at me. Then it came on to rain in the usual way, and she began to assure me between showers that you were so kind and gentle that it hurt you to work, or to work at my horrid pig-sticking business, I forget which, and I begged her pardon for having misjudged you so cruelly, and then the whole thing sort of simmered off into a discussion of whether I thought you'd rather she wore pink or blue at breakfast. So I guess you're all right. Only you'd better write quick and apologize.

I didn't get at the facts of the quarrel, but you're in the wrong. A fellow's always in the wrong when he quarrels with a woman, and even if he wasn't at the start he's sure to be before he gets through. And a man who's decided to marry can't be too quick learning to apologize for things he didn't say and to be forgiven for things he didn't do. When you differ with your wife, never try to reason out who's in the wrong, because you'll find that after you've proved it to her she'll still have a lot of talk left that she hasn't used.

Of course, it isn't natural and it isn't safe for married people, and especially young married people, not to quarrel a little, but you'll save a heap of trouble if you make it a rule never to refuse a request before breakfast and never to grant one after dinner. I don't know why it is, but most women get up in the morning as cheerful as a breakfast-food ad., while a man will snort and paw for trouble the minute his hoofs touch the floor. Then, if you'll remember that the longer the last word is kept the bitterer it gets, and that your wife is bound to have it anyway, you'll cut the rest of your quarrels so short that she'll never find out just how much meanness there is in you. Be the silent partner at home and the thinking one at the office. Do your loose talking in your sleep.

Of course, if you get a woman who's really fond of quarreling there isn't any special use in keeping still, because she'll holler if you talk back and yell if you don't. The best that you can do is to pretend that you've got a chronic case of ear-ache, and keep your ears stuffed with cotton. Then, like as not, she'll buy you one of these things that you hold in your mouth so that you can hear through your teeth.

I don't believe you're going to draw anything of that sort with Helen, but this is a mighty uncertain world, especially when you get to betting on which way the kitten is going to jump—you can usually guess right about the cat—and things don't always work out as planned.

While there's no sure rule for keeping out of trouble in this world, there's a whole set of them for getting into it.

I remember a mighty nice, careful mother who used to shudder when slang was used in her presence. So she vowed she'd give *her* son a name that the boys couldn't twist into any low, vulgar nick-name. She called him Algernon, but the kid had a pretty big nose, and the first day he was sent to school with his long lace collar and his short velvet pants the boys christened him Snooty, and now his parents are the only people who know what his real name is.

After you've been married a little while you're going to find that there are two kinds of happiness you can have—home happiness and fashionable happiness. With the first kind you get a lot of children and with the second a lot of dogs. While the dogs mind better and seem more affectionate, because they kiss you with their whole face, I've always preferred to associate with children. Then, for the first kind of happiness you keep house for yourself, and for the second you keep house for the neighbors.

You can buy a lot of home happiness with a mighty small salary, but fashionable happiness always costs just a little more than you're making. You can't keep down expenses when you've got to keep up appearances—that is, the appearance of being something that you ain't. You're in the fix of a dog chasing his tail—you can't make ends meet, and if you do it'll give you such a crick in your neck that you won't get any real satisfaction out of your gymnastics. You've got to live on a rump-steak basis when you're alone, so that you can appear to be on a quail-on-toast basis when you have company. And while they're eating your quail and betting that they're cold-storage birds, they'll be whispering to each other that the butcher told their cook that you lived all last week on a soup-bone and two pounds of Hamburger steak. Your wife must hog it around the house in an old wrapper, because she's got to have two or three of those dresses that come high on the bills and low on the shoulders, and when she wears 'em the neighbors are going to wonder how much you're short in your accounts. And if you've been raised a shouting Methodist and been used to hollering your satisfaction in a good hearty Glory! or a Hallelujah! you've got to quit it and go to one of those churches where the right answer to the question, "What is the chief end of man?" is "Dividend," and where they think you're throwing a fit and sick the sexton on to you if you forget yourself and whoop it up a little when your religion gets to working.

Then, if you do have any children, you can't send them to a plain public school to learn reading, writing, and arithmetic, because they've got to go to a fashionable private one to learn hog-Latin, hog-wash, and how much the neighbors are worth. Of course, the rich children are going to say that they're pushing little kids, but they've got to learn to push and to shove and to butt right in where they're not wanted if they intend to herd with the real angora billy-goats. They've got to learn how to bow low to every one in front of them and to kick out at every one behind them. It's been my experience that it takes a good four-year course in snubbing before you can graduate a first-class snob.

Then, when you've sweat along at it for a dozen years or so, you'll wake up some morning and discover that your appearances haven't deceived any one but yourself. A man who tries that game is a good deal like the fellow who puts on a fancy vest over a dirty shirt—he's the only person in the world who can't see the egg-spots under his chin. Of course, there isn't any real danger of your family's wearing a false front while I'm alive, because I believe Helen's got too much sense to stand for anything of the sort; but if she should, you can expect the old man around with his megaphone to whisper the real figures to your neighbors.

I don't care how much or how little money you make—I want you to understand that there's only one place in the world where you can live a happy life, and that's inside your income. A family that's living beyond its means is simply a business that's losing money, and it's bound to go to smash. And to keep a safe distance ahead of the sheriff you've got to make your wife help. More men go broke through bad management at home than at the office. And I might add that a lot of men who are used to getting only one dollar's worth of food for a five-dollar bill down-town, expect their wives to get five dollars' worth of food for a one-dollar bill at the corner grocery, and to save the change toward a pair of diamond earrings. These fellows would plant a tin can and kick because they didn't get a case of tomatoes.

Of course, some women put their husband's salaries on their backs instead of his ribs; but there are a heap more men who burn up their wives' new sealskin sacques in two-bit cigars. Because a man's a good provider it doesn't always mean that he's a good husband—it may mean that he's a hog. And when there's a cuss in the family and it comes down to betting which, on general principles the man always carries my money. I make mistakes at it, but it's the only winning system I've ever been able to discover in games of chance.

You want to end the wedding trip with a business meeting and talk to your wife quite as frankly as you would to a man whom you'd taken into partnership. Tell her just what your salary is and then lay it out between you—so much for joint expenses, the house and the housekeeping, so much for her expenses, so much for yours, and so much to be saved. That last is the one item on which you can't afford to economize. It's the surplus and undivided profits account of your business, and until the concern accumulates a big one it isn't safe to move into offices on Easy Street.

A lot of fool fathers only give their fool daughters a liberal education in spending, and it's pretty hard to teach those women the real facts about earning and saving, but it's got to be done unless you want to be the fool husband of a fool wife. These girls have an idea that men get money by going to a benevolent old party behind some brass bars and shoving a check at him and telling him that they want it in fifties and hundreds.

You should take home your salary in actual money for a while, and explain that it's all you got for sweating like a dog for ten hours a day, through six long days, and that the cashier handed it out with an expression as if you were robbing the cash-drawer of an orphan asylum. Make her understand that while those that have gets, when they present a check, those that haven't gets it in the neck. Explain that the benevolent old party is only on duty when papa's daughter has a papa that Bradstreet rates AA, and that when papa's daughter's husband presents a five-dollar check with a ten-cent overdraft, he's received by a low-browed old brute who calls for the bouncer to put him out. Tell her right at the start the worst about the butcher, and the grocer, and the iceman, and the milkman, and the plumber, and the gas-meter—that they want their money and that it has to come out of that little roll of bills. Then give her enough to pay them, even if you have to grab for your lunch from a high stool. I used to know an old Jew who said that the man who carved was always a fool or a hog, but you've got to learn not to divide your salary on either basis.

Make your wife pay cash. A woman never really understands money till she's done that for a while. I've noticed that people rarely pay down the money for foolish purchases—they charge them. And it's mighty seldom that a woman's extravagant unless she or her husband pays the bills by check. There's something about counting out the actual legal tender on the spot that keeps a woman from really wanting a lot of things which she thinks she wants.

When I married your ma, your grandpa was keeping eighteen niggers busy seeing that the family did nothing. She'd had a liberal education, which, so far as I've been able to find out, means teaching a woman everything except the real business that she's going into—that is, if she marries. But when your ma swapped the big house and the eighteen niggers for me and an old mammy to do the rough work, she left the breakfast-in-bed, fine-lady business behind her and started right in to get the rest of the education that belonged to her. She did a mighty good job, too, all except making ends meet, and they were too elastic for her at first—sort of snapped back and left a deficit just when she thought she had them together.

She was mighty sorry about it, but she'd never heard of any way of getting money except asking papa for it, and she'd sort of supposed that every one asked papa when they wanted any, and, why didn't I ask papa? I finally made her see that I couldn't ask my papa, because I hadn't any, and that I couldn't ask hers, because it was against the rules of the game as I played it, and that was her first real lesson in high finance and low finances.

I gave her the second when she came to me about the twentieth of the month and kissed me on the ear and sent a tickly little whisper after it to the effect that the household appropriation for the month was exhausted and the pork-barrel and the meal-sack and the chicken-coop were in the same enfeebled condition.

I didn't say anything at first, only looked pretty solemn, and then I allowed that she'd have to go into the hands of a receiver. Well, sir, the way she snuggled up to me and cried made me come pretty close to weakening, but finally I told her that I reckoned I could manage to be appointed by the court and hush up the scandal so the neighbors wouldn't hear of it.

I took charge of her little books and paid over to myself her housekeeping money each month, buying everything myself, but explaining every move I made, until in the end I had paid her out of debt and caught up with my salary again. Then I came home on the first of the month, handed out her share of the money, and told her that the receiver had been discharged by the court.

My! but she was pleased. And then she paid me out for the scare I'd given her by making me live on side-meat and corn-bread for a month, so she'd be sure not to get the sheriff after her again. Of course, I had to tell her all about it in the end, and though she's never forgotten what she learned about money during the receivership, she's never quite forgiven the receiver.

Speaking of receiving, I notice the receipts of hogs are pretty light. Hold your lard prices up stiff to the market. It looks to me as if that Milwaukee crowd was getting under the February delivery.

Your affectionate father,

JOHN GRAHAM.

P.S.—You've got to square me with Helen.

VI.

_____

From John Graham, at the Waldorf-Astoria, New York, to his son, Pierrepont, at the Union Stock Yards, Chicago.

The young man has written describing the magnificent wedding presents that are being received, and hinting discreetly that it would not come amiss if he knew what shape the old man's was going to take, as he needs the money.

NEW YORK, December 12, 189-.

Dear Pierrepont: These fellows at the branch house here have been getting altogether too blamed refined to suit me in their ideas of what's a fair day's work, so I'm staying over a little longer than I had intended, in order to ring the rising bell for them and to get them back into good Chicago habits. The manager started in to tell me that you couldn't do any business here before nine or ten in the morning—and I raised that boy myself!

We had a short season of something that wasn't exactly prayer, but was just as earnest, and I think he sees the error of his ways. He seemed to feel that just because he was getting a fair share of the business I ought to be satisfied, but I don't want any half-sports out gunning with me. It's the fellow that settles himself in his blind before the ducks begin to fly who gets everything that's coming to his decoys. I reckon we'll have to bring this man back to Chicago and give him a beef house where he has to report at five before he can appreciate what a soft thing it is to get down to work at eight.

I'm mighty glad to hear you're getting so many wedding

presents that you think you'll have enough to furnish your house, only you don't want to fingermark them looking to see it a hundred-thousand-dollar check from me ain't slipped in among them, because it ain't.

I intend to give you a present, all right, but there's a pretty wide margin for guessing between a hundred thousand dollars and the real figures. And you don't want to feel too glad about what you've got, either, because you're going to find out that furnishing a house with wedding presents is equivalent to furnishing it on the installment plan. Along about the time you want to buy a go-cart for the twins, you'll discover that you'll have to make Tommy's busted old baby-carriage do, because you've got to use the money to buy a tutti-frutti ice-cream spoon for the young widow who sent you a doormat with "Welcome" on it. And when she gets it, the young widow will call you that idiotic Mr. Graham, because she's going to have sixteen other tutti-frutti ice-cream spoons, and her doctor's told her that if she eats sweet things she'll have to go in the front door like a piano—sideways.

Then when you get the junk sorted over and your house furnished with it, you're going to sit down to dinner on some empty soap-boxes, with the soup in cut-glass finger-bowls, and the fish on a hand-painted smoking-set, and the meat on dinky, little egg-shell salad plates, with ice-cream forks and fruit knives to eat with. You'll spend most of that meal wondering why somebody didn't send you one of those hundred and sixteen piece five-dollar-ninety-eight-marked-down-from-six sets of china. While I don't mean to say that the average wedding present carries a curse instead of a blessing, it could usually repeat a few cuss-words if it had a retentive memory.

Speaking of wedding presents and hundred-thousand-dollar checks naturally brings to mind my old friend Hamilton Huggins—Old Ham they called him at the Yards—and the time he gave his son, Percival, a million dollars.

Take him by and large, Ham was as slick as a greased pig. Before he came along, the heft of the beef hearts went into the fertilizer tanks, but he reasoned out that they weren't really tough, but that their firmness was due to the fact that the meat in them was naturally condensed, and so he started putting them out in his celebrated condensed mincemeat at ten cents a pound. Took his pigs' livers, too, and worked 'em up into a genuine Strasburg pâté de foie gras that made the wild geese honk when they flew over his packing-house. Discovered that a little chopped cheek-meat at two cents a pound was a blamed sight healthier than chopped pork at six. Reckoned that by running twenty-five per cent. of it into his pork sausage he saved a hundred thousand people every year from becoming cantankerous old dyspeptics.

Ham was simply one of those fellows who not only have convolutions in their brains, but kinks and bow-knots as well, and who can believe that any sort of a lie is gospel truth just so it is manufactured and labeled on their own premises. I confess I ran out a line of those pigs' liver pâtés myself, but I didn't do it because I was such a patriot that I couldn't stand seeing the American flag insulted by a lot of Frenchmen getting a dollar for a ten-cent article, and that simply because geese have smaller livers than pigs.

For all Old Ham was so shrewd at the Yards, he was one of those fellows who begin losing their common-sense at the office door, and who reach home doddering and blithering. Had a fool wife with the society bug in her head, and as he had the one-of-our-leading-citizens bug in his, they managed between them to raise a lovely warning for a Sunday-school superintendent in their son, Percival.

Percy was mommer's angel boy with the sunny curls, who was to be raised a gentleman and to be "shielded from the vulgar surroundings and coarse associations of her husband's youth," and he was proud popper's pet, whose good times weren't going to be spoiled by a narrow-minded old brute of a father, or whose talents weren't going to be smothered in poverty, the way the old man's had been. No, sir-ee, Percy was going to have all the money he wanted, with the whisky bottle always in sight on the sideboard and no limit on any game he wanted to sit in, so that he'd grow up a perfect little gentleman and know how to use things instead of abusing them.

I want to say right here that I've heard a good deal of talk in my time about using whisky, and I've met a good many thousand men who bragged when they were half loaded that they could quit at any moment, but I've never met one of these fellows who would while the whisky held out. It's been my experience that when a fellow begins to brag that he can quit whenever he wants to, he's usually reached the point where he can't.

Naturally, Percy had hardly got the pap-rag out of his mouth before he learned to smoke cigarettes, and he could cuss like a little gentleman before he went into long pants. Took the four-years' sporting course at Harvard, with a postgraduate year of draw-poker and natural history—observing the habits and the speed of the ponies in their native haunts. Then, just to prove that he had paresis, Old Ham gave him a million dollars outright and a partnership in his business.

Percy started in to learn the business at the top—absorbing as much of it as he could find room for between ten and four, with two hours out for lunch—but he never got down below the frosting. The one thing that Old Ham wouldn't let him touch was the only thing about the business which really interested Percy— the speculating end of it. But everything else he did went with the old gentleman, and he was always bragging that Percy was growing up into a big, broad-gauged merchant. He got mighty mad with me when I told him that Percy was just a ready-made success who was so small that he rattled round in his seat, and that he'd better hold in his horses, as there were a good many humps in the road ahead of him.

Old Ham was a sure-thing packer, like myself, and let speculating alone, never going into the market unless he had the goods or knew where he could get them; but when he did plunge into the pit, he usually climbed out with both hands full of money and a few odd thousand-dollar bills sticking in his hair. So when

57

he came to me one day and pointed out that Prime Steam Lard at eight cents for the November delivery, and the West alive with hogs, was a crime against the consumer, I felt inclined to agree with him, and we took the bear side of the market together.

Somehow, after we had gone short a big line, the law of supply and demand quit business. There were plenty of hogs out West, and all the packers were making plenty of lard, but people seemed to be frying everything they ate, and using lard in place of hair-oil, for the Prime Steam moved out as fast as it was made. The market simply sucked up our short sales and hollered for more, like a six-months shoat at the trough. Pound away as we would, the November option moved slowly up to 8½, to 9, to 9½. Then, with delivery day only six weeks off, it jumped overnight to 10, and closed firm at 12¼. We stood to lose a little over a million apiece right there, and no knowing what the crowd that was under the market would gouge us for in the end.

As soon as 'Change closed that day, Old Ham and I got together and gave ourselves one guess apiece to find out where we stood, and we both guessed right—in a corner.

We had a little over a month to get together the lard to deliver on our short sales or else pay up, but we hadn't had enough experience in the paying-up business to feel like engaging in it. So that afternoon we wired our agents through the West to start anything that looked like a hog toward Chicago, and our men in the East to ship us every tierce of Prime Steam they could lay their hands on. Then we made ready to try out every bit of hog fat, from a grease spot up, that we could find in the country. And all the time the price kept climbing on us like a nigger going up a persimmon tree, till it was rising seventeen cents.

So far the bull crowd had managed to keep their identity hidden, and we'd been pretty modest about telling the names of the big bears, because we weren't very proud of the way we'd been caught napping, and because Old Ham was mighty anxious that Percy shouldn't know that his safe old father had been using up the exception to his rule of no speculation.

It was a near thing for us, but the American hog responded nobly—and a good many other critters as well, I suspect—and when it came on toward delivery day we found that we had the actual lard to turn over on our short contracts, and some to spare. But Ham and I had lost a little fat ourselves, and we had learned a whole lot about the iniquity of selling goods that you haven't got, even when you do it with the benevolent intention of cheapening an article to the consumer.

We got together at his office in the Board of Trade building to play off the finals with the bull crowd. We'd had inspectors busy all night passing the lard which we'd gathered together and which was arriving by boat-loads and train-loads. Then, before 'Change opened, we passed the word around through our brokers that there wasn't any big short interest left, and to prove it they pointed to the increase in the stocks of Prime Steam in store and gave out the real figures on what was still in transit. By the time the bell rang for trading on the floor we had built the hottest sort of a fire under the market, and thirty minutes after the opening the price of the November option had melted down flat to twelve cents.

We gave the bulls a breathing space there, for we knew we had them all nicely rounded up in the killing-pens, and there was no hurry. But on toward noon, when things looked about right, we jumped twenty brokers into the pit, all selling at once and offering in any sized lots for which they could find takers. It was like setting off a pack of firecrackers—biff! bang! bang! our brokers gave it to them, and when the smoke cleared away the bits of that busted corner were scattered all over the pit, and there was nothing left for us to do but to pick up our profits; for we had swung a loss of millions over to the other side of the ledger.

Just as we were sending word to our brokers to steady the market so as to prevent a bad panic and failures, the door of the private office flew open, and in bounced Mr. Percy, looking like a hound dog that had lapped up a custard pie while the cook's back was turned and is hunting for a handy bed to hide under. Had let his cigarette go out—he wore one in his face as regularly as some fellows wear a pink in their buttonhole—and it was drooping from his lower lip, instead of sticking up under his nose in the old sporty, sassy way.

"Oh, gov'ner!" he cried as he slammed the door behind him; "the market's gone to hell."

"Quite so, my son, quite so," nodded Old Ham approvingly; "it's the bottomless pit to-day, all right, all right."

I saw it coming, but it came hard. Percy sputtered and stuttered and swallowed it once or twice, and then it broke loose in:

"And oh! gov'ner, I'm caught—in a horrid hole—you've got to help me out!"

"Eh! what's that!" exclaimed the old man, losing his just-after-a-hearty-meal expression. "What's that—caught—speculating, after what I've said to you! Don't tell me that you're one of that bull crowd—Don't you dare do it, sir."

"Ye-es," and Percy's voice was scared back to a whisper; "yes; and what's more, I'm the whole bull crowd—the Great Bull they've all been talking and guessing about."

Great Scott! but I felt sick. Here we'd been, like two pebbles in a rooster's gizzard, grinding up a lot of corn that we weren't going to get any good of. I itched to go for that young man myself, but I knew this was one of those holy moments between father and son when an outsider wants to pull his tongue back into its cyclone cellar. And when I looked at Ham, I saw that no help was needed, for the old man was coming out of his twenty-five-years' trance over Percy. He didn't say a word for a few minutes, just kept boring into the young man with his eyes, and though Percy had a cheek like brass, Ham's stare went through it as easy as a two-inch bit goes into boiler-plate. Then, "Take that cigaroot out of your mouth," he bellered. "What d'ye mean by coming into my office smoking cigareets?"

Percy had always smoked whatever he blamed pleased, wherever he blamed pleased before, though Old Ham wouldn't stand for it from any one else. But because things have been allowed to go all wrong for twenty-five years, it's no reason why they should be allowed to go wrong for twenty-five years and one day; and I was mighty glad to see Old Ham rubbing the sleep out of his eyes at last.

"But, gov'ner,' Percy began, throwing the cigarette away, "I really—"

"Don't you but me; I won't stand it. And don't you call me gov'ner. I won't have your low-down street slang in my office. So you're the great bull, eh? you bull-pup! you bull in a china shop! The great bull-calf, you mean. Where'd you get the money for all this cussedness? Where'd you get the money? Tell me that. Spit it out—quick—I say."

"Well, I've got a million dollars," Percy dribbled out.

"Had a million dollars, and it was my good money," the old man moaned.

"And an interest in the business, you know."

"Yep; I oughter I s'pose you hocked that."

"Not exactly; but it helped me to raise a little money."

"You bet it helped you; but where'd you get the rest? Where'd you raise the money to buy all this cash lard and ship it abroad? Where'd you get it? You tell me that."

"Well, ah—the banks—loaned—me—a—-good deal."

"On your face."

"Not exactly that—but they thought—inferred—that you were interested with me—and without—" Percy's tongue came to a full stop when he saw the old man's face.

"Oh! they did, eh! they did, eh!" Ham exploded. "Tried to bust your poor old father, did you! Would like to see him begging his bread, would you, or piking in the bucket-shops for five-dollar bills! Wasn't satisfied with soaking him with his own million! Couldn't rest when you'd swatted him with his own business! Wanted to bat him over the head with his own credit! And now you come whining around—"

"Tried to bust your poor old father"

"But, dad—"

"Don't you dad me, dad-fetch you—don't you try any Absalom business on me. You're caught by the hair, all right, and I'm not going to chip in for any funeral expenses."

Right here I took a hand myself, because I was afraid Ham was going to lose his temper, and that's one thing you can't always pick up in the same place that you left it. So I called Ham off, and told Percy to come back in an hour with his head broker and I'd protect his trades in the meanwhile. Then I pointed out to the old man that we'd make a pretty good thing on the deal, even after we'd let Percy out, as he'd had plenty of company on the bull side that could pay up; and anyway, that the boy was a blamed sight more important than the money, and here was the chance to make a man of him.

We were all ready for Mister Percy when he came back, and Ham got right down to business.

"Young man, I've decided to help you out of this hole," he began.

Percy chippered right up. "Thank you, sir," he said.

"Yes, I'm going to help you," the old man went on. "I'm going to take all your trades off your hands and assume all your obligations at the banks."

"Thank you, sir."

"Stop interrupting when I'm talking, I'm going to take up all your obligations, and you're going to pay me three million dollars for doing it. When the whole thing's cleaned up that will probably leave me a few hundred thousand in the hole, but I'm going to do the generous thing by you."

Percy wasn't so chipper now. "But, father," he protested, "I haven't got three million dollars; and you know very well I can't possibly raise any three million dollars."

"Yes, you can," said Ham. "There's the million I gave you: that makes one. There's your interest in the business; I'll buy it back for a million: that makes two. And I'll take your note at five per cent, for the third million. A fair offer, Mr. Graham?"

"Very liberal, indeed, Mr. Huggins," I answered.

"But I won't have anything to live on, let alone any chance to pay you back, if you take my interest in the business away," pleaded Percy.

"I've thought of that, too," said his father, "and I'm going to give you a job. The experience you've had in this campaign ought to make you worth twenty-five dollars a week to us in our option department. Then you can board at home for five dollars a week, and pay ten more on your note. That'll leave you ten per for clothes and extras."

Percy wriggled and twisted and tried tears. Talked a lot of flip-flap flub-doodle, but Ham was all through with the proud-popper business, and the young man found him as full of knots as a hickory root, and with a hide that would turn the blade of an ax.

Percy was simply in the fix of the skunk that stood on the track and humped up his back at the lightning express—there was nothing left of him except a deficit and the stink he'd kicked up. And a fellow can't dictate terms with those assets. In the end he left the room with a ring in his nose.

After all, there was more in Percy than cussedness, for when he finally decided that it was a case of root hog or die with him, he turned in and rooted. It took him ten years to get back into his father's confidence and a partnership, and he was still paying on the million-dollar note when the old man died and left him his whole fortune. It would have been cheaper for me in the end if I had let the old man disinherit him, because when Percy ran that Mess Pork corner three years ago, he caught me short a pretty good line and charged me two dollars a barrel more than any one else to settle. Explained that he needed the money to wipe out the unpaid balance of a million-dollar note that he'd inherited from his father.

I simply mention Percy to show why I'm a little slow to regard members of my family as charitable institutions that I should settle endowments on. If there's one thing I like less than another, it's being regarded as a human meal-ticket. What is given to you always belongs to some one else, and if the man who gave it doesn't take it back, some fellow who doesn't have to have things given to him is apt to come along and run away with it. But what you earn is your own, and apt to return your affection for it with interest—pretty good interest.

Your affectionate father,

JOHN GRAHAM.

P.S.—I forgot to say that I had bought a house on Michigan Avenue for Helen, but there's a provision in the deed that she can turn you out if you don't behave.

VII.

From John Graham, at the Union Stock Yards, Chicago, to his son, Pierrepont, at Yemassee-on-the-Tallahassee.

The young man is now in the third quarter of the honey-moon, and the old man has decided that it is time to bring him fluttering down to earth.

CHICAGO, January 17, 189-.

Dear Pierrepont: After you and Helen had gone off looking as if you'd just bought seats on 'Change and been baptized into full membership with all the sample bags of grain that were handy, I found your new mother-in-law out in the dining-room, and, judging by the plates around her, she was carrying in stock a full line of staple and fancy groceries and delicatessen. When I struck her she was crying into her third plate of ice cream, and complaining bitterly to the butler because the mould had been opened so carelessly that some salt had leaked into it.

Of course, I started right in to be sociable and to cheer her up, but I reckon I got my society talk a little mixed—I'd been one of the pall-bearers at Josh Burton's funeral the day before—and I told her that she must bear up and eat a little something to keep up her strength, and to remember that our loss was Helen's gain.

Now, I don't take much stock in all this mother-in-law talk, though I've usually found that where there's so much smoke there's a little fire; but I'm bound to say that Helen's ma came back at me with a sniff and a snort, and made me feel sorry that I'd intruded on her sacred grief. Told me that a girl of Helen's

65

beauty and advantages had naturally been very, very popular, and greatly sought after. Said that she had been received in the very best society in Europe, and might have worn strawberry leaves if she'd chosen, meaning, I've since found out, that she might have married a duke.

Crying into her third plate of ice cream

I tried to soothe the old lady, and to restore good feeling by allowing that wearing leaves had sort of gone out of fashion with the Garden of Eden, and that I liked Helen better in white satin, but everything I said just seemed to enrage her the more. Told me plainly that she'd thought, and hinted that she'd hoped, right up to last month, that Helen was going to marry a French nobleman, the Count de Somethingerino or other, who was crazy about her. So I answered that we'd both had a narrow escape, because I'd been afraid for a year that I might wake up any morning and find myself the father-in-law of a Crystal Slipper chorus-girl. Then, as it looked as if the old lady was going to bust a corset-string in getting out her answer, I modestly slipped away, leaving her leaking brine and acid like a dill pickle that's had a bite taken out of it.

Good mothers often make bad mothers-in-law, because they usually believe that, no matter whom their daughters marry, they could have gone farther and fared better. But it struck me that Helen's ma has one of those retentive memories and weak mouths—the kind of memory that never loses anything it should forget, and the kind of mouth that can't retain a lot of language which it shouldn't lose.

Of course, you want to honor your mother-in-law, that your days may be long in the land; but you want to honor this one from a distance, for the same reason. Otherwise, I'm afraid you'll hear a good deal about that French count, and how hard it is for Helen to have to associate with a lot of mavericks from the Stock Yards, when she might be running with blooded stock on the other side. And if you glance up from your morning paper and sort of wonder out loud whether Corbett or Fitzsimmons is the better man, mother-in-law will glare at you over the top of her specs and ask if you don't think it's invidious to make any comparisons if they're both striving, to lead earnest, Christian lives. Then, when you come home at night, you'll be apt to find your wife sniffing your breath when you kiss her, to see if she can catch that queer, heavy smell which mother has noticed on it; or looking at you slant-eyed when she feels some letters in your coat, and wondering if what mother says is true, and if men who've once taken chorus-girls to supper never really recover from the habit.

On general principles, it's pretty good doctrine that two's a company and three's a crowd, except when the third is a cook. But I should say that when the third is Helen's ma it's a mob, out looking for a chance to make rough-house. A good cook, a good wife and a good job will make a good home anywhere; but you add your mother-in-law, and the first thing you know you've got two homes, and one of them is being run on alimony.

You want to remember that, beside your mother-in-law, you're a comparative stranger to your wife. After you and Helen have lived together for a year, you ought to be so well acquainted that she'll begin to believe that you know almost as much as mamma; but during the first few months of married life there are apt to be a good many tie votes on important matters, and if mother-in-law is on the premises she is generally going to break the tie by casting the deciding vote with daughter. A man can often get the best of one woman, or ten men, but not of two women, when one of the two is mother-in-law.

When a young wife starts housekeeping with her mother too handy, it's like running a business with a new manager and keeping the old one along to see how things go. It's not in human nature that the old manager, even with the best disposition in the world, shouldn't knock the new one a little, and you're Helen's new manager. When I want to make a change, I go about it like a crab—get rid of the old shell first, and then plunge right in and begin to do business with the new skin. It may be a little tender and open to attack at first, but it doesn't take long to toughen up when it finds out that the responsibility of protecting my white meat is on it.

You start a woman with sense to making mistakes and you've started her to learning common-sense; but you let some one else shoulder her natural responsibilities and keep her from exercising her brain, and it'll be fat-witted before she's forty. A lot of girls find it mighty handy to start with mother to look after the housekeeping and later to raise the baby; but by and by, when mamma has to quit, they don't understand that the butcher has to be called down regularly for leaving those heavy ends on the steak or running in the shoulder chops on you, and that when Willie has the croup she mustn't give the little darling a stiff hot Scotch, or try to remove the phlegm from his throat with a button-hook.

There are a lot of women in this world who think that there's only one side to the married relation, and that's their side. When one of them marries, she starts right out to train her husband into kind old Carlo, who'll go downtown for her every morning and come home every night, fetching a snug little basketful of money in his mouth and wagging his tail as he lays it at her feet. Then it's a pat on the head and "Nice doggie." And he's taught to stand around evenings, retrieving her gloves and handkerchief, and snapping up with a pleased licking of his chops any little word that she may throw to him. But you let him start in to have a little fun scratching and stretching himself, or pawing her, and it's "Charge, Carlo!" and "Bad doggie!"

Of course, no man ever believes when he marries that he's going to wind up as kind Carlo, who droops his head so that the children can pull his ears, and who sticks up his paw so as to make it easier for his wife to pull his leg. But it's simpler than you think.

As long as fond fathers slave and ambitious mothers sacrifice so that foolish daughters can hide the petticoats of poverty under a silk dress and crowd the doings of cheap society into the space in their heads which ought to be filled with plain, useful knowledge, a lot of girls are going to grow up with the idea that getting married means getting rid of care and responsibility instead of assuming it.

A fellow can't play the game with a girl of this sort, because she can't play fair. He wants her love and a wife; she wants a provider, not a lover, and she takes him as a husband because she can't draw his salary any other way. But she can't return his affection, because her love is already given to another; and when husband and wife both love the same person, and that person is the wife, it's usually a life sentence at hard labor for the husband. If he wakes up a little and tries to assert himself after he's been married a year or so, she shudders and sobs until he sees what a brute he is; or if that doesn't work, and he still pretends to have a little spirit, she goes off into a rage and hysterics, and that usually brings him to heel again. It's a mighty curious thing how a woman who has the appetite and instincts of a turkey—buzzard will often make her husband believe that she's as high-strung and delicate as a canary-bird!

It's been my experience that both men and women can fool each other before marriage, and that women can keep right along fooling men after marriage, but that as soon as the average man gets married he gets found out. After a woman has lived in the same house with a man for a year, she knows him like a good merchant knows his stock, down to any shelf-worn and slightly damaged morals which he may be hiding behind fresher goods in the darkest corner of his immortal soul. But even if she's married to a fellow who's so mean that he'd take the pennies off a dead man's eyes (not because he needed the money, but because he hadn't the change handy for a two-cent stamp), she'll never own up to the worst about him, even to herself, till she gets him into a divorce court.

I simply mention these things in a general way. Helen has shown signs of loving you, and you've never shown any symptoms of hating yourself, so I'm not really afraid that you're going to get the worst of it now. So far as I can see, your mother-in-law is the only real trouble that you have married. But don't you make the mistake of criticizing her to Helen or of quarrelling with her. I'll attend to both for the family. You simply want to dodge when she leads with the right, take your full ten seconds on the floor, and come back with your left cheek turned toward her, though, of course, you'll yank it back out of reach just before she lands on it. There's nothing like using a little diplomacy in this world, and, so far as women are concerned, diplomacy is knowing when to stay away. And a diplomatist is one who lets the other fellow think he's getting his way, while all the time *he's* having his own. It never does any special harm to let people have their way with their mouths.

What you want to do is to keep mother-in-law from mixing up in your family affairs until after she gets used to the disgrace of having a pork-packer for a son-in-law, and Helen gets used to pulling in harness with you. Then mother'll mellow up into a nice old lady who'll brag about you to the neighbors. But until she gets to this point, you've got to let her hurt your feelings without hurting hers. Don't you ever forget that Helen's got a mother-in-law, too, and that it's some one you think a heap of.

Whenever I hear of a fellow's being found out by his wife, it always brings to mind the case of Dick Hodgkins, whom I knew when I was a young fellow, back in Missouri. Dickie was one of a family of twelve, who all ran a little small any way you sized them up, and he was the runt. Like most of these little fellows, when he came to match up for double harness, he picked out a six-footer, Kate Miggs. Used to call her Honeybunch, I remember, and she called him Doodums.

Honeybunch was a good girl, but she was as strong as a six-mule team, and a cautious man just naturally shied away from her. Was a pretty free stepper in the mazes of the dance, and once, when she was balancing partners with Doodums, she kicked out sort of playful to give him a love pat and fetched him a clip with her tootsey that gave him water on the kneepan. It ought to have been a warning to Doodums, but he was plumb infatuated, and went around pretending that he'd been kicked by a horse. After that the boys used to make Honeybunch mighty mad when she came out of dark corners with Doodums, by feeling him to see if any of his ribs were broken. Still he didn't take the hint, and in the end she led him to the altar.

We started in to give them a lovely shivaree after the wedding, beginning with a sort of yell which had been invented by the only fellow in town who had been to college.

As I remember, it ran something like this:

Hun, hun, hunch!
Bun, bun, bunch!
Funny, funny!
Honey, honey!
Funny Honeybunch!

But as soon as we got this off, and before we could begin on the dishpan chorus, Honeybunch came at us with a couple of bed-slats and cleaned us all out.

Before he had married, Doodums had been one of half a dozen half-baked sports who drank cheap whisky and played expensive poker at the Dutchman's; and after he'd held Honeybunch in his lap evenings for a month, he reckoned one night that he'd drop down street and look in on the boys. Honeybunch reckoned not, and he didn't press the matter, but after they'd gone to bed and she'd dropped off to sleep, he slipped into his clothes and down the waterspout to the ground. He sat up till two o'clock at the Dutchman's, and naturally, the next morning he had a breath like a gasoline runabout, and looked as if he'd been attending a successful coon-hunt in the capacity of the coon.

Honeybunch smelt his breath and then she smelt a mouse, but she wasn't much of a talker and she didn't ask any questions—of him. But she had brother Jim make some inquiries, and a few days later, when Doodums complained of feeling all petered out and wanted to go to bed early, she was ready for him.

Honeybunch wasn't any invalid, and when she went to bed it was to sleep, so she rigged up a simple little device in the way of an alarm and dropped off peacefully, while Doodums pretended to.

When she began to snore in her upper register and to hit the high C, he judged the coast was clear, and leaped lightly out of bed. Even before he'd struck the floor he knew there'd been a horrible mistake somewhere, for he felt a tug as if he'd hooked a hundred-pound catfish. There was an awful ripping and tearing sound, something fetched loose, and his wife was sitting up in bed blinking at him in the moonlight. It seemed that just before she went to sleep she'd pinned her nightgown to his with a safety pin, which wasn't such a bad idea for a simple, trusting, little village maiden.

"Was you wantin' anything, Duckie Doodums?" she asked in a voice like the running of sap in maple-sugar time.

"N-n-nothin' but a drink of water, Honeybunch sweetness," he stammered back.

"N-n-nothin' but a drink of water"

"You're sure you ain't mistook in your thirst and that it ain't a suddint cravin' for licker, and that you ain't sort of p'intin' down the waterspout for the Dutchman's, Duckie Doodums?"

"Shorely not, Honeybunch darlin'," he finally fetched up, though he was hardly breathing.

"Because your ma told me that you was given to somnambulasticatin' in your sleep, and that I must keep you tied up nights or you'd wake up some mornin' at the foot of a waterspout with your head bust open and a lot of good licker spilt out on the grass."

"Don't you love your Doodums anymore?" was all Dickie could find to say to this; but Honeybunch had too much on her mind to stop and swap valentines just then.

"You wouldn't deceive your Honeybunch, would you, Duckie Doodums?"

"I shorely would not."

"Well, don't you do it, Duckie Doodums, because it would break my heart; and if you should break my heart I'd just naturally bust your head. Are you listenin', Doodums?"

Doodums was listening.

"Then you come back to bed and stay there."

Doodums never called his wife Honeybunch after that. Generally it was Kate, and sometimes it was Kitty, and when she wasn't around it was usually Kitty-cat. But he minded better than anything I ever met on less than four legs.

Your affectionate father,

JOHN GRAHAM.

P.S.—You might tear up this letter.

VIII.

From John Graham, at the Union Stock Yards, Chicago, to his son, Pierrepont, at Yemassee-on-the-Tallahassee.

In replying to his father's hint that it is time to turn his thoughts from love to lard, the young man has quoted a French sentence, and the old man has been both pained and puzzled by it.

CHICAGO, January 24, 189-.

Dear Pierrepont: I had to send your last letter to the fertilizer department to find out what it was all about. We've got a clerk there who's an Oxford graduate, and who speaks seven languages for fifteen dollars a week, or at the rate of something more than two dollars a language. Of course, if you're such a big thinker that your ideas rise to the surface too fast for one language to hold 'em all, it's a mighty nice thing to know seven; but it's been my experience that seven spread out most men so thin that they haven't anything special to say in any of them. These fellows forget that while life's a journey, it isn't a palace-car trip for most of us, and that if they hit the trail packing a lot of weight for which they haven't any special use, they're not going to get very far. You learn men and what men should do, and how they should do it, and then if you happen to have any foreigners working for you, you can hire a fellow at fifteen per to translate hustle to 'em into their own fool language. It's always been my opinion that everybody spoke American while the tower of Babel was building, and that the Lord let the good people keep right on speaking it. So when you've got anything to say to me, I want you to say it in language that will grade regular on the Chicago Board of Trade.

Some men fail from knowing too little, but more fail from knowing too much, and still more from knowing it all. It's a mighty good thing to understand French if you can use it to some real purpose, but when all the good it does a fellow is to help him understand the foreign cuss-words in a novel, or to read a story which is so tough that it would make the Queen's English or any other ladylike language blush, he'd better learn hog-Latin! He can be just the same breed of yellow dog in it, and it don't take so much time to pick it up.

Never ask a man what he knows, but what he can do. A fellow may know everything that's happened since the Lord started the ball to rolling, and not be able to do anything to help keep it from stopping. But when a man can do anything, he's bound to know something worth while. Books are all right, but dead men's brains are no good unless you mix a live one's with them.

It isn't what a man's got in the bank, but what he's got in his head, that makes him a great merchant. Rob a miser's safe and he's broke; but you can't break a big merchant with a jimmy and a stick of dynamite. The first would have to start again just where he began—hoarding up pennies; the second would have his principal assets intact. But accumulating knowledge or piling up money, just to have a little more of either than the next fellow, is a fool game that no broad-gauged man has time enough to sit in. Too much learning, like too much money, makes most men narrow.

I simply mention these things in a general way. You know blame well that I don't understand any French, and so when you spring it on me you are simply showing a customer the wrong line of goods. It's like trying to sell our Pickled Luncheon Tidbits to a fellow in the black belt who doesn't buy anything but plain dry-salt hog in hunks and slabs. It makes me a little nervous for fear you'll be sending out a lot of letters to the trade some day, asking them if their stock of Porkuss Americanuss isn't running low.

The world is full of bright men who know all the right things to say and who say them in the wrong place. A young fellow always thinks that if he doesn't talk he seems stupid, but it's better to shut up and seem dull than to open up and prove yourself a fool. It's a pretty good rule to show your best goods last.

Whenever I meet one of those fellows who tells you all he knows, and a good deal that he doesn't know, as soon as he's introduced to you, I always think of Bill Harkness, who kept a temporary home for broken-down horses—though he didn't call it that—back in Missouri. Bill would pick up an old critter whose par value was the price of one horse-hide, and after it had been pulled and shoved into his stable, the boys would stand around waiting for crape to be hung on the door. But inside a week Bill would be driving down Main Street behind that horse, yelling Whoa! at the top of his voice while it tried to kick holes in the dashboard.

Bill had a theory that the Ten Commandments were suspended while a horse-trade was going on, so he did most of his business with strangers. Caught a Northerner nosing round his barn one day, and inside of ten minutes the fellow was driving off behind what Bill described as "the peartest piece of ginger and cayenne in Pike County." Bill just made a free gift of it to the Yankee, he said, but to keep the transaction from being a piece of pure charity he accepted fifty dollars from him.

The stranger drove all over town bragging of his bargain, until some one casually called his attention to the fact that the mare was stone-blind. Then he hiked back to Bill's and went for him in broken Bostonese, winding up with:

"What the skip-two-and-carry-one do you mean, you old hold-your-breath-and-take-ten-swallows, by stealing my good money. Didn't you know the horse was blind? Why didn't you tell me?"

"Yep," Bill bit off from his piece of store plug; "I reckon I knew the hoss was blind, but you see the feller I bought her of"—and he paused to settle his chaw—"asked me not to mention it. You wouldn't have me violate a confidence as affected the repertashun of a pore dumb critter, and her of the opposite sect, would you?" And the gallant Bill turned scornfully away from the stranger.

There were a good many holes in Bill's methods, but he never leaked information through them; and when I come across a fellow who doesn't mention it when he's asked not to, I come pretty near letting him fix his own salary. It's only a mighty big man that doesn't care whether the people whom he meets believe that he's big; but the smaller a fellow is, the bigger he wants to appear. He hasn't anything of his own in his head that's of any special importance, so just to prove that he's a trusted employee, and in the confidence of the boss, he gives away everything he knows about the business, and, as that isn't much, he lies a little to swell it up. It's a mighty curious thing how some men will lie a little to impress people who are laughing at them; will drink a little in order to sit around with people who want to get away from them; and will even steal a little to "go into society" with people who sneer at them.

The most important animal in the world is a turkey-cock. You let him get among the chickens on the manure pile behind the barn, with his wings held down stiff, his tail feathers stuck up starchy, his wish-bone poked out perky, and gobbling for room to show his fancy steps, and he's a mighty impressive fowl. But a small boy with a rock and a good aim can make him run a mile. When you see a fellow swelling up and telling his firm's secrets, holler Cash! and you'll stampede him back to his hall bedroom.

I dwell a little on this matter of loose talking, because it breaks up more firms and more homes than any other one thing I know. The father of lies lives in Hell, but he spends a good deal of his time in Chicago. You'll find him on the Board of Trade when the market's wobbling, saying that the Russians are just about to eat up Turkey, and that it'll take twenty million bushels of our wheat to make the bread for the sandwich; and down in the street, asking if you knew that the cashier of the Teenth National was leading a double life as a single man in the suburbs and a singular life for a married man in the city; and out on Prairie Avenue, whispering that it's too bad Mabel smokes Turkish cigarettes, for she's got such pretty curly hair; and how sad it is that Daisy and Dan are going to separate, 'but they do say that he—sh! sh! hush; here she comes." Yet, when you come to wash your pan of dirt, and the lies have all been carried off down the flume, and you've got the color of the few particles of solid, eighteen-carat truth left, you'll find it's the Sultan who's smoking Turkish cigarettes; and that Mabel is trying cubebs for her catarrh; and that the cashier of the Teenth National belongs to a whist club in the suburbs and is the superintendent of a Sunday-school in the city; and that Dan has put Daisy up to visiting her mother to ward off a threatened swoop down from the old lady; and that the Czar hasn't done a blame thing except to become the father of another girl baby.

It's pretty hard to know how to treat a lie when it's about yourself. You can't go out of your way to deny it, because that puts you on the defensive; and sending the truth after a lie that's got a running start is like trying to round up a stampeded herd of steers while the scare is on them. Lies are great travellers, and welcome visitors in a good many homes, and no questions asked. Truth travels slowly, has to prove its identity, and then a lot of people hesitate to turn out an agreeable stranger to make room for it.

About the only way I know to kill a lie is to live the truth. When your credit is doubted, don't bother to deny the rumors, but discount your bills. When you are attacked unjustly, avoid the appearance of evil, but avoid also the appearance of being too good—that is, better than usual. A man can't be too good, but he can appear too good. Surmise and suspicion feed on the unusual, and when a man goes about his business along the usual rut, they soon fade away for lack of nourishment. First and last every fellow gets a lot of unjust treatment in this world, but when he's as old as I am and comes to balance his books with life and to credit himself with the mean things which weren't true that have been said about him, and to debit himself with the mean things which were true that people didn't get on to or overlooked, he'll find that he's had a tolerably square deal. This world has some pretty rotten spots on its skin, but it's sound at the core.

There are two ways of treating gossip about other people, and they're both good ways. One is not to listen to it, and the other is not to repeat it. Then there's young Buck Pudden's wife's way, and that's better than either, when you're dealing with some of these old heifers who browse over the range all day, stuffing themselves with gossip about your friends, and then round up at your house to chew the cud and slobber fake sympathy over you.

Buck wasn't a bad fellow at heart, for he had the virtue of trying to be good, but occasionally he would walk in slippery places. Wasn't very sure-footed, so he fell down pretty often, and when he fell from grace it usually cracked the ice. Still, as he used to say, when he shot at the bar mirrors during one of his periods of temporary elevation, he paid for what he broke—cash for the mirrors and sweat and blood for his cussedness.

Then one day Buck met the only woman in the world—a mighty nice girl from St. Jo—and she was hesitating over falling in love with him, till the gossips called to tell her that he was a dear, lovely fellow, and wasn't it too bad that he had such horrid habits? That settled it, of course, and she married him inside of thirty days, so that she could get right down to the business of reforming him.

I don't, as a usual thing, take much stock in this marrying men to reform them, because a man's always sure of a woman when he's married to her, while a woman's never really afraid of losing a man till she's got him. When you want to teach a dog new tricks, it's all right to show him the biscuit first, but you'll usually get better results by giving it to him after the performance. But Buck's wife fooled the whole town and almost put the gossips out of business by keeping Buck straight for a year. She allowed that what he'd been craving all the time was a home and family, and that his rare-ups came from not having 'em. Then, like most reformers, she overdid it—went and had twins. Buck thought he owned the town, of course, and that would have been all right if he hadn't included the saloons among his real estate. Had to take his drinks in pairs, too, and naturally, when he went home that night and had another look at the new arrivals, he thought they were quadruplets.

Buck straightened right out the next day, went to his wife and told her all about it, and that was the last time he ever had to hang his head when he talked to her, for he never took another drink. You see, she didn't reproach him, or nag him—simply said that she was mighty proud of the way he'd held on for a year, and that she knew she could trust him now for another ten. Man was made a little lower than the angels, the Good Book says, and I reckon that's right; but he was made a good while ago, and he hasn't kept very well. Yet there are a heap of women in this world who are still right in the seraphim class. When your conscience doesn't tell you what to do in a matter of right and wrong, ask your wife.

Naturally, the story of Buck's final celebration came to the gossips like a thousand-barrel gusher to a drilling outfit that's been finding dusters, and they went one at a time to tell Mrs. Buck all the dreadful details and how sorry they were for her. She would just sit and listen till they'd run off the story, and hemstitched it, and embroidered it, and stuck fancy rosettes all over it. Then she'd smile one of those sweet baby smiles that women give just before the hair-pulling begins, and say:

"Law, Mrs. Wiggleford"—the deacon's wife was the one who was condoling with her at the moment—"people will talk about the best of us. Seems as if no one is safe nowadays. Why, they lie about the deacon, even. I know it ain't true, and you know it ain't true, but only yesterday somebody was trying to tell me that it was right strange how a professor and a deacon got that color in his beak, and while it might be inflammatory veins or whatever he claimed it was, she reckoned that, if he'd let some one else tend the alcohol barrel, he wouldn't have to charge up so much of his stock to leakage and evaporation."

Of course, Mrs. Buck had made up the story about the deacon, because every one knew that he was too mean to drink anything that he could sell, but by the time Buck's wife had finished, Mrs. Wiggleford was so busy explaining and defending him that she hadn't any further interest in Buck's case. And each one that called was sent away with a special piece of home scandal which Mrs. Buck had invented to keep her mind from dwelling on her neighbor's troubles.

She followed up her system, too, and in the end it got so that women would waste good gossip before they'd go to her with it. For if the pastor's wife would tell her "as a true friend" that the report that she had gone to the theatre in St. Louis was causing a scandal, she'd thank her for being so sweetly thoughtful, and ask if nothing was sacred enough to be spared by the tongue of slander, though she, for one, didn't believe that there was anything in the malicious talk that the Doc was cribbing those powerful Sunday evening discourses from a volume of Beecher's sermons. And when they'd press her for the name of her informant, she'd say: "No, it was a lie; she knew it was a lie, and no one who sat under the dear pastor would believe it; and they mustn't dignify it by noticing it." As a matter of fact, no one who sat under Doc Pottle would have believed it, for his sermons weren't good enough to have been cribbed; and if Beecher could have heard one of them he would have excommunicated him.

Buck's wife knew how to show goods. When Buck himself had used up all the cuss-words in Missouri on his conduct, she had sense enough to know that his stock of trouble was full, and that if she wanted to get a hold on him she mustn't show him stripes, but something in cheerful checks. Yet when the trouble-hunters looked her up, she had a full line of samples of their favorite commodity to show them.

I simply mention these things in a general way. Seeing would naturally be believing, if cross-eyed people were the only ones who saw crooked, and hearing will be believing when deaf people are the only ones who don't hear straight. It's a pretty safe rule, when you hear a heavy yarn about any one, to allow a fair amount for tare, and then to verify your weights.

Your affectionate father,

JOHN GRAHAM.

P.S.—I think you'd better look in at a few of the branch houses on your way home and see if you can't make expenses.

IX.

From John Graham, at the Union Stock Yards, Chicago, to his son, Pierrepont, care of Graham & Company's brokers, Atlanta.

Following the old man's suggestion, the young man has rounded out the honeymoon into a harvest moon, and is sending in some very satisfactory orders to the house.

CHICAGO, February 1, 189-.

Dear Pierrepont: Judging from the way the orders are coming in, I reckon that you must be lavishing a little of your surplus ardor on the trade. So long as you are in such good practise, and can look a customer in the eye and make him believe that he's the only buyer you ever really loved, you'd better not hurry home too fast. I reckon Helen won't miss you for a few hours every day, but even if she should it's a mighty nice thing to be missed, and she's right there where you can tell her every night that you love her just the same; while the only way in which you can express your unchanged affection for the house is by sending us lots of orders. If you do that you needn't bother to write and send us lots of love.

The average buyer is a good deal like the heiress to a million dollars who's been on the market for eight or ten years, not because there's no demand for her, but because there's too much. Most girls whose capital of good looks is only moderate, marry, and marry young, because they're like a fellow on 'Change who's scalping the market—not inclined to take chances, and always ready to make a quick turn. Old maids are usually the girls who were so homely that they never had an offer, or so good-looking that they carried their matrimonial corner from one option to another till the new crop came along and bust them. But a girl with a million dollars isn't a speculative venture. She can advertise for sealed proposals on her fiftieth birthday and be oversubscribed like an issue of 10 per cent. Government bonds. There's no closed season on heiresses, and, naturally, a bird that can't stick its head up without getting shot at becomes a pretty wary old fowl.

A buyer is like your heiress—he always has a lot of nice young drummers flirting and fooling around him, but mighty few of them are so much in earnest that they can convince him that their only chance for happiness lies in securing his particular order. But you let one of these dead-in-earnest boys happen along, and the first thing you know he's persuaded the heiress that he loves her for herself alone or has eloped from town with an order for a car-load of lard.

A lot of young men start off in business with an idea that they must arm themselves with the same sort of weapons that their competitors carry. There's nothing in it. Fighting the devil with fire is all foolishness, because that's the one weapon with which he's more expert than any one else. I usually find that it's pretty good policy to oppose suspicion with candor, foxiness with openness, indifference with earnestness. When you deal squarely with a crooked man you scare him to death, because he thinks you're springing some new and extra-deep game on him.

A fellow who's subject to cramps and chills has no business in the water, but if you start to go in swimming, go in all over. Don't be one of those chappies who prance along the beach, shivering and showing their skinny shapes, and then dabble their feet in the surf, pour a little sand in their hair, and think they've had a bath.

You mustn't forget, though, that it's just as important to know when to come out as when to dive in. I mention this because yesterday some one who'd run across you at Yemassee told me that you and Helen were exchanging the grip of the third degree under the breakfast-table, and trying to eat your eggs with your left hands. Of course, this is all very right and proper if you can keep it up, but I've known a good many men who would kiss their wives on the honeymoon between swallows of coffee and look like an ass a year later when she chirruped out at the breakfast-table, "Do you love me, darling?" I'm just a little afraid that you're one of those fellows who wants to hold his wife in his lap during the first six months of his married life, and who, when she asks him at the end of a year if he loves her, answers "Sure." I may be wrong about this, but I've noticed a tendency on your part to slop over a little, and a pail that slops over soon empties itself.

Exchanging the grip of the third degree

It's been my experience that most women try to prove their love by talking about it, and most men by spending money. But when a pocketbook or a mouth is opened too often nothing but trouble is left in it.

Don't forget the little attentions due your wife, but don't hurt the grocer's feelings or treat the milkman with silent contempt in order to give them to her. You can hock your overcoat before marriage to buy violets for a girl, but when she has the run of your wardrobe you can't slap your chest and explain that you stopped wearing it because you're so warm-blooded. A sensible woman soon begins to understand that affection can be expressed in porterhouse steaks as well as in American beauties. But when Charlie, on twenty-five a week, marries a fool, she pouts and says that he doesn't love her just the same because he takes her to the theatre now in the street-cars, instead of in a carriage, as he used to in those happy days before they were married. As a matter of fact, this doesn't show that she's losing Charlie's love, but that he's getting his senses back. It's been my experience that no man can really attend to business properly when he's chased to the office every morning by a crowd of infuriated florists and livery-men.

Of course, after a girl has spent a year of evenings listening to a fellow tell her that his great ambition is to make her life one grand, sweet song, it jars her to find the orchestra grunting and snoring over the sporting extra some night along six months after the ceremony. She stays awake and cries a little over this, so when he sees her across the liver and bacon at breakfast, he forgets that he's never told her before that she could look like anything but an angel, and asks, "Gee, Mame, what makes your nose so red?" And that's the place where a young couple begins to adjust itself to life as it's lived on Michigan Avenue instead of in the story-books.

There's no rule for getting through the next six months without going back to mamma, except for the Brute to be as kind as he knows how to be and the Angel as forgiving as she can be. But at the end of that time a boy and girl with the right kind of stuff in them have been graduated into a man and a woman. It's only calf love that's always bellering about it. When love is full grown it has few words, and sometimes it growls them out.

I remember, when I was a youngster, hearing old Mrs. Hoover tell of the trip she took with the Doc just after they were married. Even as a young fellow the Doc was a great exhorter. Knew more Scripture when he was sixteen than the presiding elder. Couldn't open his mouth without losing a verse. Would lose a chapter when he yawned.

Well, when Doc was about twenty-five, he fell in love with a mighty sweet young girl, Leila Hardin, who every one said was too frivolous for him. But the Doc only answered that it was his duty to marry her to bring her under Christian influences, and they set off down the river to New Orleans on their honeymoon.

Mrs. Hoover used to say that he hardly spoke to her on the trip. Sat around in a daze, scowling and rolling his eyes, or charged up and down the deck, swinging his arms and muttering to himself. Scared her half to death, and she spent all her time crying when he wasn't around. Thought he didn't love her any more, and it wasn't till the first Sunday after she got home that she discovered what had ailed him. Seemed that in the exaltation produced by his happiness at having got her, he'd been composing a masterpiece, his famous sermon on the Horrors of Hell, that scared half of Pike County into the fold, and popularized dominoes with penny points as a substitute for dollar-limit draw-poker among those whom it didn't quite fetch.

Curious old cuss, the Doc. Found his wife played the piano pretty medium rotten, so when he wanted to work himself into a rage about something he'd sit down in the parlor and make her pound out "The Maiden's Prayer."

It's a mighty lucky thing that the Lord, and not the neighbors, makes the matches, because Doc's friends would have married him to Deacon Dody's daughter, who was so chuck full of good works that there was no room inside her for a heart. She afterward eloped with a St. Louis drummer, and before he divorced her she'd become the best lady poker player in the State of Missouri. But with Leila and the Doc it was a case of give-and-take from the start—that is, as is usual with a good many married folks, she'd give and he'd take. There never was a better minister's wife, and when you've said that you've said the last word about good wives and begun talking about martyrs, because after a minister's wife has pleased her husband she's got to please the rest of the church.

I simply mention Doc's honeymoon in passing as an example

of the fact that two people can start out in life without anything in common apparently, except a desire to make each other happy, and, with that as a platform to meet on, keep coming closer and closer together until they find that they have everything in common. It isn't always the case, of course, but then it's happened pretty often that before I entered the room where an engaged couple were sitting I've had to cough or whistle to give them a chance to break away; and that after they were married I've had to keep right on coughing or whistling for the same couple to give them time to stop quarreling.

There are mighty few young people who go into marriage with any real idea of what it means. They get their notion of it from among the clouds where they live while they are engaged, and, naturally, about all they find up there is wind and moonshine; or from novels, which always end just before the real trouble begins, or if they keep on, leave out the chapters that tell how the husband finds the rent and the wife the hired girls. But if there's one thing in the world about which it's possible to get all the facts, it's matrimony. Part of them are right in the house where you were born, and the neighbors have the rest.

It's been my experience that you've got to have leisure to be unhappy. Half the troubles in this world are imaginary, and it takes time to think them up. But it's these oftener than the real troubles that break a young husband's back or a young wife's heart.

A few men and more women can be happy idle when they're single, but once you marry them to each other they've got to find work or they'll find trouble. Everybody's got to raise something in this world, and unless people raise a job, or crops, or children, they'll raise Cain. You can ride three miles on the trolley car to the Stock Yards every morning and find happiness at the end of the trip, but you may chase it all over the world in a steam yacht without catching up with it. A woman can find fun from the basement to the nursery of her own house, but give her a license to gad the streets and a bunch of matinée tickets and she'll find discontent. There's always an idle woman or an idle man in every divorce case. When the man earns the bread in the sweat of his brow, it's right that the woman should perspire a little baking it.

There are two kinds of discontent in this world—the discontent that works and the discontent that wrings its hands. The first gets what it wants, and the second loses what it has. There's no cure for the first but success; and there's no cure at all for the second, especially if a woman has it; for she doesn't know what she wants, and so you can't give it to her.

Happiness is like salvation—a state of grace that makes you enjoy the good things you've got and keep reaching out, for better ones in the hereafter. And home isn't what's around you, but what's inside you.

I had a pretty good illustration of this whole thing some years ago when a foolish old uncle died and left my cellar boss, Mike Shaughnessy, a million dollars. I didn't bother about it particularly, for he'd always been a pretty level-headed old Mick, and I supposed that he'd put the money in pickle and keep right along at his job. But one morning, when he came rooting and grunting into my office in a sort of casual way, trying to keep a plug hat from falling off the back of his head, I knew that he was going to fly the track. Started in to tell me that his extensive property interests demanded all his attention now, but I cut it short with:

"Mike, you've been a blamed good cellar boss, but you're going to make a blamed bad millionaire. Think it over."

Well, sir, I'm hanged if that fellow, whom I'd raised from the time he was old enough to poke a barrel along the runways with a pointed stick, didn't blow a cloud of cigar smoke in my face to show that he was just as big as I was, and start tight in to regularly cuss me out. But he didn't get very far. I simply looked at Mm, and said sudden, "Git, you Mick," and he wilted back out of the office just as easy as if he hadn't had ten cents.

I heard of him off and on for the next year, putting up a house on Michigan Avenue, buying hand-painted pictures by the square foot and paying for them by the square inch—for his wife had decided that they must occupy their proper station in society—and generally building up a mighty high rating as a good thing.

As you know, I keep a pretty close eye on the packing house, but on account of my rheumatism I don't often go through the cellars. But along about this time we began to get so many complaints about our dry salt meats that I decided to have a little peek at our stock for myself, and check up the new cellar boss. I made for him and his gang first, and I was mightily pleased, as I came upon him without his seeing me, to notice how he was handling his men. No hollering, or yelling, or cussing, but every word counting and making somebody hop. I was right upon him before I discovered that it wasn't the new foreman, but Mike, who was bossing the gang. He half ducked behind a pile of Extra Short Clears when he saw me, but turned, when he found that it was too late, and faced me bold as brass.

"A nice state you've let things get in while I was away, sorr," he began.

It was Mike, the cellar boss, who knew his job, and no longer Mr. Shaughnessy, the millionaire, who didn't know his, that was talking, so I wasn't too inquisitive, and only nodded.

"Small wonder," he went on, "that crime's incr'asing an' th' cotton crop's decreasing in the black belt, when you're sendin' such mate to the poor naygurs. Why don't you git a cellar man that's been raised with the hogs, an' 'll treat 'em right when they're dead?"

"I'm looking for one," says I.

"I know a likely lad for you," says he.

"Report to the superintendent," says I; and Mike's been with me ever since. I found out when I looked into it that for a week back he'd been paying the new cellar boss ten dollars a day to lay around outside while he bossed his job.

Mike sold his old masters to a saloon-keeper and moved back to Packingtown, where he invested all his money in houses, from which he got a heap of satisfaction, because, as his tenants were compatriots, he had plenty of excitement collecting his rents. Like most people who fall into fortunes suddenly, he had bought a lot of things, not because he needed them or really wanted them, but because poorer people couldn't have them. Yet in the end he had sense enough to see that happiness can't be inherited, but that it must be earned.

Being a millionaire is a trade like a doctor's—you must work up through every grade of earning, saving, spending and giving, or you're no more fit to be trusted with a fortune than a quack with human life. For there's no trade in the world, except the doctor's, on which the lives and the happiness of so many people depend as the millionaire's; and I might add that there's no other in which there's so much malpractice.

Your affectionate father,

JOHN GRAHAM.

X.

From John Graham, at Mount Clematis, Michigan, to his son, Pierrepont, at the Union Stock Yards, Chicago.

The young man has done famously during the first year of his married life, and the old man has decided to give him a more important position.

MOUNT CLEMATIS, January 1, 1900.

Dear Pierrepont: Since I got here, my rheumatism has been so bad mornings that the attendant who helps me dress has had to pull me over to the edge of the bed by the seat of my pajamas. If they ever give way, I reckon I'll have to stay in bed all day. As near as I can figure out from what the doctor says, the worse you feel during the first few days you're taking the baths, the better you really are. I suppose that when a fellow dies on their hands they call it a cure.

I'm by the worst of it for to-day, though, because I'm downstairs. Just now the laugh is on an old boy with benevolent side-whiskers, who's sliding down the balusters, and a fat old party, who looks like a bishop, that's bumping his way down with his feet sticking out straight in front of him. Shy away from these things that end in an ism, my boy. From skepticism to rheumatism they've an ache or a pain in every blamed joint.

Still, I don't want to talk about my troubles, but about your own. Barton leaves us on the first, and so we shall need a new assistant general manager for the business. It's a ten-thousand-dollar job, and a nine-thousand-nine-hundred-and-ninety-nine-dollar man can't fill it. From the way in which you've handled your department during the past year, I'm inclined to think that you can deliver that last dollar's worth of value. Anyway, I'm going to try you, and you've got to make good, because if you should fail it would be a reflection on my judgment as a merchant and a blow to my pride as a father. I could bear up under either, but the combination would make me feel like firing you.

As a matter of fact, I can't make you general manager; all I can do is to give you the title of general manager. And a title is like a suit of clothes—it must fit the man who tries to wear it. I can clothe you in a little brief authority, as your old college friend, Shakespeare, puts it, but I can't keep people from laughing at you when they see you swelling around in your high-water pants.

It's no use demanding respect in this world; you've got to command it. There's old Jim Wharton, who, for acting as a fourth-class consul of a fifth-class king, was decorated with the order of the garter or the suspender or the eagle of the sixth class—the kind these kings give to the cook when he gets just the right flavor of garlic in a fancy sauce. Jim never did a blame thing in his life except to inherit a million dollars from a better man, who happened to come over on the Cunard Line instead of the Mayflower, but he'd swell around in our best society, with that ribbon on his shirt-front, thinking that he looked like Prince Rupert by Louis the Fourteenth and Lady Clara Vere de Vere, instead of the fourth assistant to the floor manager at the Plumbers' ball. But you take Tom Lipton, who was swelled up into Sir Thomas because he discovered how to pack a genuine Yorkshire ham in Chicago, and a handle looks as natural on him as on a lard pail.

A man is a good deal like a horse—he knows the touch of a master, and no matter how lightly the reins are held over him, he understands that he must behave. But let a fellow who isn't quite sure of himself begin sawing on a horse's mouth, and the first thing you know the critter bucks and throws him.

You've only one pair of eyes with which to watch 10,000

men, so unless they're open all the time you'll be apt to overlook something here and there; but you'll have 10,000 pairs of eyes watching you all the time, and they won't overlook anything. You mustn't be known as an easy boss, or as a hard boss, but as a just boss. Of course, some just men lean backward toward severity, and some stoop down toward mercy. Both kinds may make good bosses, but I've usually found that when you hold the whip hand it's a great thing not to use the whip.

It looks like a pretty large contract to know what 10,000 men are doing, but, as a matter of fact, there's nothing impossible about it. In the first place, you don't need to bother very much about the things that are going all right, except to try to make them go a little better; but you want to spend your time smelling out the things that are going all wrong and laboring with them till you've persuaded them to lead a better life. For this reason, one of the most important duties of your job is to keep track of everything that's out of the usual. If anything unusually good happens, there's an unusually good man behind it, and he ought to be earmarked for promotion; and if anything unusually bad happens, there's apt to be an unusually bad man behind that, and he's a candidate for a job with another house.

A good many of these things which it's important for you to know happen a little before beginning and a little after quitting time; and so the real reason why the name of the boss doesn't appear on the time-sheet is not because he's a bigger man than any one else in the place, but because there shouldn't be any one around to take his time when he gets down and when he leaves.

You can tell a whole lot about your men from the way in which they come in and the way in which they go home; but because a fellow is in the office early, it doesn't always mean that he's panting to begin work; it may mean that he's been out all night. And when you see a fellow poring over his books after the others have quit, it doesn't always follow that he's so wrapped up in his work that he can't tear himself away from it. It may mean that during business hours he had his head full of horse-racing instead of figures, and that he's staying to chase up the thirty cents which he's out in his balance. You want to find out which.

The extra-poor men and the extra-good men always stick their heads up above the dead-level of good-enough men; the first to holler for help, and the second to get an extra reach. And when your attention is attracted to one of these men, follow him up and find out just what sort of soil and fertilizer he needs to grow fastest. It isn't enough to pick likely stock; you've got to plant it where the conditions are right to develop its particular possibilities. A fellow who's got the making of a five-thousand-dollar office man in him may not sell enough lard to fry a half-portion of small potatoes if you put him on the road. Praise judiciously given may act on one man like an application of our bone-meal to a fruit tree, and bring out all the pippins that are in the wood; while in the other it may simply result in his going all to top.

You mustn't depend too much on the judgment of department heads and foremen when picking men for promotion. Take their selection if he is the best man, but know for yourself that he is the best man.

Sometimes a foreman will play a favorite, and, as any fellow who's been to the races knows, favorites ain't always winners. And sometimes, though not often, he'll try to hold back a good man through jealousy. When I see symptoms of a foreman's being jealous of a man under him, that fellow doesn't need any further recommendation to me. A man's never jealous of inferiority.

It's a mighty valuable asset for a boss, when a vacancy occurs in a department, to be able to go to its head when he recommends Bill Smith for the position, and show that he knows all about Bill Smith from his number-twelve socks up to his six-and-a-quarter hat, and to ask: "What's the matter with Tom Jones for the job?" When you refuse to take something just as good in this world, you'll usually find that the next time you call the druggist has the original Snicker's Sassafras Sneezer in stock.

It's mighty seldom, though, that a really good man will

complain to you that he's being held down, or that his superior is jealous of him. It's been my experience that it's only a mighty small head that so small an idea as this can fill. When a fellow has it, he's a good deal like one of those girls with the fatal gift of beauty in her imagination, instead of her face—always believing that the boys don't dance with her because the other girls tell them spiteful things about her.

Besides always having a man in mind for any vacancy that may occur, you want to make sure that there are two men in the office who understand the work of each position in it. Every business should be bigger than any one man. If it isn't, there's a weak spot in it that will kill it in the end. And every job needs an understudy. Sooner or later the star is bound to fall sick, or get the sulks or the swelled head, and then, if there's no one in the wings who knows her lines, the gallery will rotten-egg the show and howl for its money back. Besides, it has a mighty chastening and stimulating effect on the star to know that if she balks there's a sweet young thing in reserve who's able and eager to go the distance.

Of course, I don't mean by this that you want to play one man against another or try to minimize to a good man his importance to the house. On the contrary, you want to dwell on the importance of all positions, from that of office-boy up, and make every man feel that he is a vital part of the machinery of the business, without letting him forget that there's a spare part lying around handy, and that if he breaks or goes wrong it can be fitted right in and the machine kept running. It's good human nature to want to feel that something's going to bust when you quit, but it's bad management if things are fixed so that anything can.

In hiring new men, you want to depend almost altogether on your own eyes and your own judgment. Remember that when a man's asking for a job he's not showing you himself, but the man whom he wants you to hire. For that reason, I never take on an applicant after a first interview. I ask him to call again. The second time he may not be made up so well, and he may have forgotten some of his lines. In any event, hell feel that he knows you a little better, and so act a little easier and talk a little freer.

Very often a man whom you didn't like on his first appearance will please you better on his second, because a lot of people always appear at their worst when they're trying to appear at their best. And again, when you catch a fellow off guard who seemed all right the first time, you may find that he deaconed himself for your benefit, and that all the big strawberries were on top. Don't attach too much importance to the things which an applicant has a chance to do with deliberation, or pay too much attention to his nicely prepared and memorized speech about himself. Watch the little things which he does unconsciously, and put unexpected questions which demand quick answers.

If he's been working for Dick Saunders, it's of small importance what Dick says of him in his letter of recommendation. If you want Dick's real opinion, get it in some other way than in an open note, of which the subject's the bearer. As a matter of fact, Dick's opinion shouldn't carry too much weight, except on a question of honesty, because if Dick let him go, he naturally doesn't think a great deal of him; and if the man resigned voluntarily, Dick is apt to feel a little sore about it. But your applicant's opinion of Dick Saunders is of very great importance to you. A good man never talks about a real grievance against an old employer to a new one; a poor man always pours out an imaginary grievance to any one who will listen. You needn't cheer in this world when you don't like the show, but silence is louder than a hiss.

Hire city men and country men; men who wear grandpa's Sunday suit; thread-bare men and men dressed in those special four-ninety-eight bargains; but don't hire dirty men. Time and soap will cure dirty boys, but a full-grown man who shrinks from the use of water externally is as hard to cure as one who avoids its use internally. It's a mighty curious thing that you can tell a man his morals are bad and he needs to get religion, and hell still remain your friend; but that if you tell him his linen's dirty and he needs to take a bath, you've made a mortal enemy.

Give the preference to the lean men and the middleweights. The world is full of smart and rich fat men, but most of them got their smartness and their riches before they got their fat.

Always appoint an hour at which you'll see a man, and if he's late a minute don't bother with him. A fellow who can be late when his own interests are at stake is pretty sure to be when yours are. Have a scribbling pad and some good letter paper on a desk, and ask the applicant to write his name and address. A careful and economical man will use the pad, but a careless and wasteful fellow will reach for the best thing in sight, regardless of the use to which it's to be put.

Look in a man's eyes for honesty; around his mouth for weakness; at his chin for strength; at his hands for temperament; at his nails for cleanliness. His tongue will tell you his experience, and under the questioning of a shrewd employer prove or disprove its statements as it runs along. Always remember, in the case of an applicant from another city, that when a man says he doesn't like the town in which he's been working it's usually because he didn't do very well there.

You want to be just as careful about hiring boys as men. A lot of employers go on the theory that the only important thing about a boy is his legs, and if they're both fitted on and limber they hire him. As a matter of fact, a boy is like a stick of dynamite, small and compact, but as full of possibilities of trouble as a car-load of gunpowder. One bad boy in a Sunday-school picnic can turn it into a rough-house outfit for looting orchards, and one little cuss in your office can demoralize your kids faster than you can fire them.

I remember one boy who organized a secret society, called the Mysterious League. It held meetings in our big vault, which they called the donjon keep, and, naturally, when one of them was going on, boys were scarcer around the office than hen's teeth. The object of the league, as I shook it out of the head leaguer by the ear, was to catch the head bookkeeper, whom the boys didn't like, and whom they called the black caitiff, alone in the vault some night while he was putting away his books, slam the door, and turn the combination on him. Tucked away in a corner of the vault, they had a message for him, written in red ink, on a sheep's skull, telling him to tremble, that he was in the hands of the Mysterious League, and that he would be led at midnight to the torture chamber. I learned afterward that when the bookkeeper had reached in his desk to get a pen, a few days before, he had pulled out a cold, clammy, pickled pig's foot, on which was printed: "Beware! first you will lose a leg!"

I simply mention the Mysterious League in passing. Of course, boys will be boys, but you mustn't let them be too cussed boyish during business hours. A slow boy can waste a lot of the time of a five-thousand-dollar man whose bell he's answering; and a careless boy can mislay a letter or drop a paper that will ball up the work of the most careful man in the office.

It's really harder to tell what you're getting when you hire a boy than when you hire a man. I found that out for keeps a few years ago, when I took on the Angel Child. He was the son of rich parents, who weren't quite rich enough to buy chips and sit in the game of the no-limit millionaires. So they went in for what they called the simple life. I want to say right here that I'm a great believer in the simple life, but some people are so blamed simple about it that they're idiotic. The world is full of rich people who talk about leading the simple life when they mean the stingy life. They are the kind that are always giving poorer people a chance to chip in an even share with them toward defraying the expenses of the charities and the entertainments which they get up. They call it "affording those in humbler walks an opportunity to keep up their self-respect," but what they really mean is that it helps them to keep down their own expenses.

The Angel Child's mother was one of these women who talk to people that aren't quite so rich as she in the tone of one who's commending a worthy charity; but who hangs on the words of a richer woman like a dog that hopes a piece of meat is going to be thrown at it, and yet isn't quite sure that it won't get a kick instead. As a side-line, she made a specialty of trying to uplift the masses, and her husband furnished the raw material for the uplifting, as he paid his men less and worked 'em harder than any one else in Chicago.

Well, one day this woman came into my office, bringing her only son with her. He was a solemn little cuss, but I didn't get much chance to size him up, because his ma started right in to explain how he'd been raised—no whipping, no—but I cut it short there, and asked her to get down to brass tacks, as I was very busy trying to see that 70,000,000 people were supplied with their daily pork. So she explained that she wanted me to give the Angel Child a job in my office during his summer vacation, so that he could see how the other half lived, and at the same time begin to learn self-reliance.

I was just about to refuse, when it occurred to me that if he had never really had a first-class whipping it was a pity not to put him in the way of getting one. So I took him by the hand and led him to headquarters for whippings, the bench in the shipping department, where a pretty scrappy lot of boys were employed to run errands, and told the boss to take him on.

I wasn't out of hearing before one kid said, "I choose him," and another, whom they called the Breakfast-Food Baby, because he was so strong, answered, "Naw; I seen him first."

I dismissed the matter from my mind then, but a few days later, when I was walking through the shipping department, it occurred to me that I might as well view the remains of the Angel Child, if they hadn't been removed to his late residence. I found him sitting in the middle of the bench, looking a little sad and lonesome, but all there. The other boys seemed to be giving him plenty of room, and the Breakfast-Food Baby, with both eyes blacked, had edged along to the end of the bench. I beckoned to the Angel Child to follow me to my private office.

"What does this mean, young man?" I asked, when he got there. "Have you been fighting?"

"Yes, sir," he answered, sort of brightening up.

"Which one?"

"Michael and Patrick the first day, sir."

"Did you lick 'em?"

"I had rather the better of it," he answered, as precise as a slice of cold-boiled Boston.

"And the second?"

"Why, the rest of 'em, sir."

"Including the Breakfast-Food—er, James?"

He nodded. "James is very strong, sir, but he lacks science. He drew back as if he had a year to hit me, and just as he got good and ready to strike, I pasted him one in the snoot, and followed that up with a left jab in the eye."

I hadn't counted on boxing lessons being on the bill of fare of the simple life, and it raised my hopes still further to see from that last sentence how we had grafted a little Union Stock Yards on his Back Bay Boston. In fact, my heart quite warmed to the lad; but I looked at him pretty severely, and only said:

"Mark you, young man, we don't allow any fighting around here; and if you can't get along without quarrelling with the boys in the shipping department, I'll have to bring you into these offices, where I can have an eye on your conduct."

There were two or three boys in the main office who were spoiling for a thrashing, and I reckoned that the Angel Child would attend to their cases; and he did. He was cock of the walk in a week, and at the same time one of the bulliest, daisiest, most efficient, most respectful boys that ever worked for me. He put a little polish on the other kids, and they took a little of the extra shine off him. He's in Harvard now, but when he gets out there's a job waiting for him, if he'll take it.

That was a clear case of catching an angel on the fly, or of entertaining one unawares, as the boy would have put it, and it taught me not to consider my prejudices or his parents in hiring a boy, but to focus my attention on the boy himself, when he was the one who would have to run the errands. The simple life was a pose and pretense with the Angel Child's parents, and so they were only a new brand of snob; but the kid had been caught young and had taken it all in earnest; and so he was a new breed of boy, and a better one than I'd ever hired before.

Your affectionate father,

JOHN GRAHAM.

XI.

From John Graham, at Mount Clematis, Michigan, to his son, Pierrepont, at the Union Stock Yards, Chicago.

The young man has sent the old man a dose of his own medicine, advice, and he is proving himself a good doctor by taking it.

MOUNT CLEMATIS, January 25, 1900.

Dear Pierrepont: They've boiled everything out of me except the original sin, and even that's a little bleached, and they've taken away my roll of yellow-backs, so I reckon they're about through with me here, for the present. But instead of returning to the office, I think I'll take your advice and run down to Florida for a few weeks and have a "try at the tarpon," as you put it. I don't really need a tarpon, or want a tarpon, and I don't know what I could do with a tarpon if I hooked one, except to yell at him to go away; but I need a burned neck and a peeled nose, a little more zest for my food, and a little more zip about my work, if the interests of the American hog are going to be safe in my hands this spring. I don't seem to have so much luck as some fellows in hooking these fifty-pound fish lies, but I always manage to land a pretty heavy appetite and some big nights' sleep when I strike salt water. Then I can go back to the office and produce results like a hen in April with eggs at eleven cents a dozen.

Health is like any inheritance—you can spend the interest in work and play, but you mustn't break into the principal. Once you do, and it's only a matter of time before you've got to place the remnants in the hands of a doctor as receiver; and receivers are mighty partial to fees and mighty slow to let go. But if you don't work with him to get the business back on a sound basis there's no such thing as any further voluntary proceedings, and the remnants become remains.

I don't really need a tarpon ...
but I need a burned neck and a peeled nose

It's a mighty simple thing, though, to keep in good condition, because about everything that makes for poor health has to get into you right under your nose. Yet a fellow'll load up with pie and buckwheats for breakfast and go around wondering about his stomach-ache, as if it were a put-up job that had been played on him when he wasn't looking; or he'll go through his dinner pickling each course in a different brand of alcohol, and sob out on the butler's shoulder that the booze isn't as pure as it used to be when he was a boy; or he'll come home at midnight singing "The Old Oaken Bucket," and act generally as if all the water in the world were in the well on the old homestead, and the mortgage on that had been foreclosed; or from 8 P.M. to 3 G.X.

he'll sit in a small game with a large cigar, breathing a blend of light-blue cigarette smoke and dark-blue cuss-words, and next day, when his heart beats four and skips two, and he has that queer, hopping sensation in the knees, he'll complain bitterly to the other clerks that this confining office work is killing him.

Of course, with all the care in the world, a fellow's likely to catch things, but there's no sense in sending out invitations to a lot of miscellaneous microbes and pretending when they call that it's a surprise party. Bad health hates a man who is friendly with its enemies—hard work, plain food, and pure air. More men die from worry than from overwork; more stuff themselves to death than die of starvation; more break their necks falling down the cellar stairs than climbing mountains. If the human animal reposed less confidence in his stomach and more in his legs, the streets would be full of healthy men walking down to business. Remember that a man always rides to his grave; he never walks there.

When I was a boy, the only doubt about the food was whether there would be enough of it; and there wasn't any doubt at all about the religion. If the pork barrel was full, father read a couple of extra Psalms at morning prayers, to express our thankfulness; and if it was empty, he dipped into Job for half an hour at evening prayers, to prove that we were better off than some folks. But you don't know what to eat these days, with one set of people saying that only beasts eat meat, and another that only cattle eat grain and green stuff; or what to believe, with one crowd claiming that there's nothing the matter with us, as the only matter that we've got is in our minds; and another crowd telling us not to mind what the others say, because they've got something the matter with their minds. I reckon that what this generation really needs is a little less pie and a little more piety.

I dwell on this matter of health, because when the stomach and liver ain't doing good work, the brain can't. A good many men will say that it's none of your business what they do in their own time, but you want to make it your business, so long as it affects what they do in your time. For this reason, you should never hire men who drink after office hours; for it's their time that gets the effects, and your time that gets the after-effects. Even if a boss grants that there's fun in drinking, it shouldn't take him long to discover that he's getting the short end of it, when all the clerks can share with him in the morning is the head and the hangover.

I might add that I don't like the effects of drinking any more than the after-effects; and for this reason you should never hire men who drink during business hours. When a fellow adds up on whisky, he's apt to see too many figures; and when he subtracts on beer, he's apt to see too few.

It may have been the case once that when you opened up a bottle for a customer he opened up his heart, but booze is a mighty poor salesman nowadays. It takes more than a corkscrew to draw out a merchant's order. Most of the men who mixed their business and their drinks have failed, and the new owners take their business straight. Of course, some one has to pay for the drinks that a drummer sets up. The drummer can't afford it on his salary; the house isn't really in the hospitality business; so, in the end, the buyer always stands treat. He may not see it in his bill for goods, but it's there, and the smart ones have caught on to it.

After office hours, the number of drinks a fellow takes may make a difference in the result to his employer, but during business hours the effect of one is usually as bad as half a dozen. A buyer who drinks hates a whisky breath when he hasn't got one himself, and a fellow who doesn't drink never bothers to discover whether he's being talked to by a simple or a compound breath. He knows that some men who drink are unreliable, and that unreliable men are apt to represent unreliable houses and to sell unreliable goods, and he hasn't the time or the inclination to stop and find out that this particular salesman has simply had a mild snort as an appetizer and a gentle soother as a digester. So he doesn't get an order, and the house gets a black eye. This is a very, very busy world, and about the only person who is really interested in knowing just how many a fellow has had is his wife, and she won't always believe him.

Naturally, when you expect so much from your men, they have a right to expect a good deal from you. If you want them to feel that your interests are theirs, you must let them see that their interests are yours. There are a lot of fellows in the world who are working just for glory, but they are mostly poets, and you needn't figure on finding many of them out at the Stock Yards. Praise goes a long way with a good man, and some employers stop there; but cash goes the whole distance, and if you want to keep your growing men with you, you mustn't expect them to do all the growing. Small salaries make slow workers and careless clerks; because it isn't hard to get an underpaid job. But a well-paid man sticketh closer than a little brother-in-law-to-be to the fellow who brings the candy. For this reason, when I close the books at the end of the year, I always give every one, from the errand boys up, a bonus based on the size of his salary and my profits. There's no way I've ever tried that makes my men take an interest in the size of my profits like giving them a share. And there's no advertisement for a house like having its men going around blowing and bragging because they're working for it.

Again, if you insist that your men shan't violate the early-closing ordinance, you must observe one yourself. A man who works only half a day Saturday can usually do a day and half's work Monday. I'd rather have my men hump themselves for nine hours than dawdle for ten.

Of course, the world is full of horses who won't work except with the whip, but that's no reason for using it on those who will. When I get a critter that hogs my good oats and then won't show them in his gait, I get rid of him. He may be all right for a fellow who's doing a peddling business, but I need a little more speed and spirit in mine.

A lot of people think that adversity and bad treatment is the test of a man, and it is—when you want to develop his strength; but prosperity and good treatment is a better one when you want to develop his weakness. By keeping those who show their appreciation of it and firing those who don't, you get an office full of crackerjacks.

While your men must feel all the time that they've got a boss who can see good work around a corner, they mustn't be allowed to forget that there's no private burying-ground on the premises for mistakes. When a Western town loses one of its prominent citizens through some careless young fellow's letting his gun go off sudden, if the sheriff buys a little rope and sends out invitations to an inquest, it's apt to make the boys more reserved about exchanging repartee; and if you pull up your men sharp when you find them shooting off their mouths to customers and getting gay in their correspondence, it's sure to cut down the mortality among our old friends in the trade. A clerk's never fresh in letters that the boss is going to see.

The men who stay in the office and plan are the brains of your business; those who go out and sell are its arms; and those who fill and deliver the orders are its legs. There's no use in the brains scheming and the arms gathering in, if the legs are going to deliver the goods with a kick.

That's another reason why it's very important for you to be in the office early. You can't personally see every order filled, and tell whether it was shipped promptly and the right goods sent, but when the telegrams and letters are opened, you can have all the kicks sorted out, and run through them before they're distributed for the day. That's where you'll meet the clerk who billed a tierce of hams to the man who ordered a box; the shipper who mislaid Bill Smith's order for lard, and made Bill lose his Saturday's trade through the delay; the department head who felt a little peevish one morning and so wrote Hardin & Co., who buy in car-lots, that if they didn't like the smoke of the last car of Bacon Short Clears they could lump it, or words to that effect; and that's where you'll meet the salesman who played a sure thing on the New Orleans track and needs twenty to get to the next town, where his check is waiting. Then, a little later, when you make the rounds of the different departments to find out how it happened, the heads will tell you all the good news that was in the morning's mail.

Of course, you can keep track of your men in a sneaking way that will make them despise you, and talk to them in a nagging spirit that will make them bristle when they see you. But it's your right to know and your business to find out, and if you collect your information in an open, frank manner, going at it in the spirit of hoping to find everything all right, instead of wanting to find something all wrong; and if you talk to the responsible man with an air of "here's a place where we can get together and correct a weakness in our business"—not my business—instead of with an "Ah! ha! I've-found-you-out" expression, your men will throw handsprings for your good opinion. Never nag a man tinder any circumstances; fire him.

A good boss, in these days when profits are pared down to the quick, can't afford to have any holes, no matter how small, in his management; but there must be give enough in his seams so that every time he stoops down to pick up a penny he won't split his pants. He must know how to be big, as well as how to be small.

Some years ago, I knew a firm who did business under the name of Foreman & Sowers. They were a regular business vaudeville team—one big and broad-gauged in all his ideas; the other unable to think in anything but boys' and misses' sizes. Foreman believed that men got rich in dollars; Sowers in cents. Of course, you can do it in either way, but the first needs brains and the second only hands. It's been my experience that the best way is to go after both the dollars and the cents.

Well, sir, these fellows launched a specialty, a mighty good thing, the Peep o' Daisy Breakfast Food, and started in to advertise. Sowers wanted to use inch space and sell single cases; Foreman kicked because full pages weren't bigger and wanted to sell in car-lots, leaving the case trade to the jobbers. Sowers only half-believed in himself, and only a quarter in the food, and only an eighth in advertising. So he used to go home nights and lie awake with a living-picture exhibit of himself being kicked out of his store by the sheriff; and out of his house by the landlord; and, finally, off the corner where he was standing with his hat out for pennies, by the policeman. He hadn't a big enough imagination even to introduce into this last picture a sport dropping a dollar bill into his hat. But Foreman had a pretty good opinion of himself, and a mighty big opinion of the food, and he believed that a clever, well-knit ad. was strong enough to draw teeth. So he would go home and build steam-yachts and country places in his sleep.

Naturally, the next morning, Sowers would come down haggard and gloomy, and grow gloomier as he went deeper into the mail and saw how small the orders were. But Foreman would start out as brisk and busy as a humming-bird, tap the advertising agent for a new line of credit on his way down to the office, and extract honey and hope from every letter.

Sowers begged him, day by day, to stop the useless fight and save the remains of their business. But Foreman simply laughed. Said there wouldn't be any remains when he was ready to quit. Allowed that he believed in cremation, anyway, and that the only way to fix a brand on the mind of the people was to burn it in with money.

Sowers worried along a few days more, and then one night, after he had been buried in the potter's field, he planned a final stroke to stop Foreman, who, he believed, didn't know just how deep in they really were. Foreman was in a particular jolly mood the next morning, for he had spent the night bidding against Pierrepont Morgan at an auction sale of old masters; but he listened patiently while Sowers called off the figures in a sort of dirge-like singsong, and until he had wailed out his final note of despair, a bass-drum crash, which he thought would bring Foreman to a realizing sense of their loss, so to speak.

"That," Sowers wound up, "makes a grand total of $800,000 that we have already lost."

Foreman's head drooped, and for a moment he was deep in thought, while Sowers stood over him, sad, but triumphant, in the feeling that he had at last brought this madman to his senses, now that his dollars were gone.

"Eight hundred thou!" the senior partner repeated mechanically. Then, looking up with a bright smile, he exclaimed: "Why, old man, that leaves us two hundred thousand still to spend before we hit the million mark!"

They say that Sowers could only gibber back at him; and Foreman kept right on and managed some way to float himself on to the million mark. There the tide turned, and after all these years it's still running his way; and Sowers, against his better judgment, is a millionaire.

I simply mention Foreman in passing. It would be all foolishness to follow his course in a good many situations, but there's a time to hold on and a time to let go, and the limit, and a little beyond, is none too far to play a really good thing. But in business it's quite as important to know how to be a good quitter as a good fighter. Even when you feel that you've got a good thing, you want to make sure that it's good enough, and that you're good enough, before you ask to have the limit taken off. A lot of men who play a nice game of authors get their feelings hurt at whist, and get it in the neck at poker.

You want to have the same principle in mind when you're handling the trade. Sometimes you'll have to lay down even when you feel that your case is strong. Often you'll have to yield a point or allow a claim when you know you're dead right and the other fellow all wrong. But there's no sense in getting a licking on top of a grievance.

Another thing that helps you keep track of your men is the habit of asking questions. Your thirst for information must fairly make your tongue loll out. When you ask the head of the canning department what we're netting for two-pound Corned Beef on the day's market for canners, and he has to say, "Wait a minute and I'll figure it out," or turn to one of his boys and ask, "Bill, what are twos netting us?" he isn't sitting close enough to his job, and, perhaps, if Bill were in his chair, he'd be holding it in his lap; or when you ask the chief engineer how much coal we burned this month, as compared with last, and why in thunder we burned it, if he has to hem and haw and say he hasn't had time to figure it out yet, but he thinks they were running both benches in the packing house most of the time, and he guesses this and reckons that, he needs to get up a little more steam himself. In short, whenever you find a fellow that ought to know every minute where he's at, but who doesn't know what's what, he's pretty likely to be *It*. When you're dealing with an animal like the American hog, that carries all its profit in the tip of its tail, you want to make sure that your men carry all the latest news about it on the tip of the tongue.

It's not a bad plan, once in a while, to check up the facts and figures that are given you. I remember one lightning calculator I had working for me, who would catch my questions hot from the bat, and fire back the answers before I could get into position to catch. Was a mighty particular cuss. Always worked everything out to the sixth decimal place. I had just about concluded he ought to have a wider field for his talents, when I asked him one day how the hams of the last week's run had been averaging in weight. Answered like a streak; but it struck me that for hogs which had been running so light they were giving up pretty generously. So I checked up his figures and found 'em all wrong. Tried him with a different question every day for a week. Always answered quick, and always answered wrong. Found that he was a base-ball rooter and had been handing out the batting averages of the Chicagos for his answers. Seems that when I used to see him busy figuring with his pencil he was working out where Anson stood on the list. He's not in Who's Who in the Stock Yards any more, you bet.

Your affectionate father,

JOHN GRAHAM.

XII.

_____

From John Graham, at Magnolia Villa, on the Florida Coast, to his son, Pierrepont, at the Union Stock Yards, Chicago.

The old man has started back to Nature, but he hasn't gone quite far enough to lose sight of his business altogether.

MAGNOLIA VILLA, February 5, 1900.

Dear Pierrepont: Last week I started back to Nature, as you advised, but at the Ocean High Roller House I found that I had to wear knee-breeches, which was getting back too far, or creases in my trousers, which wasn't far enough. So we've taken this little place, where there's nothing between me and Nature but a blue shirt and an old pair of pants, and I reckon that's near enough.

I'm getting a complexion and your ma's losing hers. Hadn't anything with her but some bonnets, so just before we left the hotel she went into a little branch store, which a New York milliner runs there, and tried to buy a shade hat.

"How would this pretty little shepherdess effect do?" asked the girl who was showing the goods, while she sized me up to see if the weight of my pocketbook made my coat sag.

"How much is it?" asked your ma.

"Fifty dollars," said the girl, as bright and sassy as you please.

"I'm not such a simple little shepherdess as that," answered your ma, just a little brighter and a little sassier, and she's going around bareheaded. She's doing the cooking and making the beds, because the white girls from the North aren't willing to do

114

"both of them works," and the native niggers don't seem to care a great deal about doing any work. And I'm splitting the wood for the kitchen stove, and an occasional fish that has committed suicide. This morning, when I was casting through the surf, a good-sized drum chased me up on shore, and he's now the star performer in a chowder that your ma has billed for dinner.

They call this place a villa, though it's really a villainy; and what I pay for it rent, though it's actually a robbery. But they can have the last bill in the roll if they'll leave me your ma, and my appetite, and that tired feeling at night. It's the bulliest time we've had since the spring we moved into our first little cottage back in Missouri, and raised climbing-roses and our pet pig, Toby. It's good to have money and the things that money will buy, but it's good, too, to check up once in a while and make sure you haven't lost the things that money won't buy. When a fellow's got what he set out for in this world, he should go off into the woods for a few weeks now and then to make sure that he's still a man, and not a plug-hat and a frock-coat and a wad of bills.

You can't do the biggest things in this world unless you can handle men; and you can't handle men if you're not in sympathy with them; and sympathy begins in humility. I don't mean the humility that crawls for a nickel in the street and cringes for a thousand in the office; but the humility that a man finds when he goes gunning in the woods for the truth about himself. It's the sort of humility that makes a fellow proud of a chance to work in the world, and want to be a square merchant, or a good doctor, or an honest lawyer, before he's a rich one. It makes him understand that while life is full of opportunities for him, it's full of responsibilities toward the other fellow, too.

That doesn't mean that you ought to coddle idleness, or to be slack with viciousness, or even to carry on the pay-roll well-meaning incompetence. For a fellow who mixes business and charity soon finds that he can't make any money to give to charity; and in the end, instead of having helped others, he's only added himself to the burden of others. The kind of sympathy

I mean holds up men to the bull-ring without forgetting in its own success the hardships and struggles and temptations of the fellow who hasn't got there yet, but is honestly trying to. There's more practical philanthropy in keeping close to these men and speaking the word that they need, or giving them the shove that they deserve, than in building an eighteen-hole golf course around the Stock Yards for them. Your force can always find plenty of reasons for striking, without your furnishing an extra one in the poor quality of the golf-balls that you give them. So I make it a rule that everything I hand out to my men shall come in the course of business, and be given on a business basis. When profits are large, they get a large bonus and a short explanation of the business reasons in the office and the country that have helped them to earn it; when profits are small, the bonus shrinks and the explanation expands. I sell the men their meats and give them their meals in the house restaurant at cost, but nothing changes hands between us except in exchange for work or cash.

If you want a practical illustration of how giving something for nothing works, pick out some one who has no real claim on you—an old college friend who's too strong to work, or a sixteenth cousin who's missed connections with the express to Fortune—and say: "You're a pretty good fellow, and I want to help you; after this I'm going to send you a hundred dollars the first of every month, until you've made a new start." He'll fairly sicken you with his thanks for that first hundred; he'll call you his generous benefactor over three or four pages for the second; he'll send you a nice little half-page note of thanks for the third; he'll write, "Yours of the first with inclosure to hand—thanks," for the fourth; he'll forget to acknowledge the fifth; and when the sixth doesn't come promptly, he'll wire collect: "Why this delay in sending my check—mail at once." And all the time he won't have stirred a step in the direction of work, because he'll have reasoned, either consciously or unconsciously: "I can't get a job that will pay me more than a hundred a month to start with; but I'm already drawing a hundred without working; so what's the use?" But when a fellow can't get a free pass, and he has any sort of stuff in him, except what hoboes are made of, he'll usually hustle for his car fare, rather than ride through life on the bumpers of a freight.

The only favor that a good man needs is an opportunity to do the best work that's in him; and that's the only present you can make him once a week that will be a help instead of a hindrance to him. It's been my experience that every man has in him the possibility of doing well some one thing, no matter how humble, and that there's some one, in some place, who wants that special thing done. The difference between a fellow who succeeds and one who fails is that the first gets out and chases after the man who needs him, and the second sits around waiting to be hunted up.

When I was a boy, we were brought up to believe that we were born black with original sin, and that we bleached out a little under old Doc Hoover's preaching. And in the church down Main Street they taught that a lot of us were predestined to be damned, and a few of us to be saved; and naturally we all had our favorite selections for the first bunch. I used to accept the doctrine of predestination for a couple of weeks every year, just before the Main Street church held its Sunday-school picnic, and there are a few old rascals in the Stock Yards that make me lean toward it sometimes now; but, in the main, I believe that most people start out with a plenty of original goodness.

The more I deal in it, the surer I am that human nature is all off the same critter, but that there's a heap of choice in the cuts. Even then a bad cook will spoil a four-pound porterhouse, where a good one will take a chuck steak, make a few passes over it with seasoning and fixings, and serve something that will line your insides with happiness. Circumstances don't make men, but they shape them, and you want to see that those under you are furnished with the right set of circumstances.

Every fellow is really two men—what he is and what he might be; and you're never absolutely sure which you're going to bury till he's dead. But a man in your position can do a whole

117

lot toward furnishing the officiating clergyman with beautiful examples, instead of horrible warnings. The great secret of good management is to be more alert to prevent a man's going wrong than eager to punish him for it. That's why I centre authority and distribute checks upon it. That's why I've never had any Honest Old Toms, or Good Old Dicks, or Faithful Old Harrys handling my good money week-days and presiding over the Sabbath-school Sundays for twenty years, and leaving the old man short a hundred thousand, and the little ones short a superintendent, during the twenty-first year.

It's right to punish these fellows, but a suit for damages ought to lie against their employers. Criminal carelessness is a bad thing, but the carelessness that makes criminals is worse. The chances are that, to start with, Tom and Dick were honest and good at the office and sincere at the Sunday-school, and that, given the right circumstances, they would have stayed so. It was their employers' business to see that they were surrounded by the right circumstances at the office and to find out whether they surrounded themselves with them at home.

A man who's fundamentally honest is relieved instead of aggrieved by having proper checks on his handling of funds. And the bigger the man's position and the amount that he handles, the more important this is. A minor employee can take only minor sums, and the principal harm done is to himself; but when a big fellow gets into you, it's for something big, and more is hurt than his morals and your feelings.

I dwell a little on these matters, because I want to fix it firmly in your mind that the man who pays the wages must put more in the weekly envelope than money, if he wants to get his full money's worth. I've said a good deal about the importance of little things to a boss; don't forget their importance to your men. A thousand-dollar clerk doesn't think with a ten-thousand-dollar head; a fellow whose view is shut in by a set of ledgers can't see very far, and so stampedes easier than one whose range is the whole shop; a brain that can't originate big things can't forget trifles so quick as one in which the new ideas keep crowding out the old annoyances. Ten thousand a year will sweeten a multitude of things that don't taste pleasant, but there's not so much sugar in a thousand to help them down. The sting of some little word or action that wouldn't get under your skin at all, is apt to swell up one of these fellows' bump of self-esteem as big as an egg-plant, and make it sore all over.

It's always been my policy to give a little extra courtesy and consideration to the men who hold the places that don't draw the extra good salaries. It's just as important to the house that they should feel happy and satisfied as the big fellows. And no man who's doing his work well is too small for a friendly word and a pat on the back, and no fellow who's doing his work poorly is too big for a jolt that will knock the nonsense out of him.

You can't afford to give your men a real grievance, no matter how small it is; for a man who's got nothing to occupy thin but his work can accomplish twice as much as one who's busy with his work and a grievance. The average man will leave terrapin and champagne in a minute to chew over the luxury of feeling abused. Even when a man isn't satisfied with the supply of real grievances which life affords, and goes off hunting up imaginary ones, like a blame old gormandizing French hog that leaves a full trough to root through the woods for truffles, you still want to be polite; for when you fire a man there's no good reason for doing it with a yell.

Noise isn't authority, and there's no sense in ripping and roaring and cussing around the office when things don't please you. For when a fellow's given to that, his men secretly won't care a cuss whether he's pleased or not. They'll jump when he speaks, because they value their heads, not his good opinion. Indiscriminate blame is as bad as undiscriminating praise—it only makes a man tired.

I learned this, like most of the sense I've got—hard; and it was only a few years ago that I took my last lesson in it. I came down one morning with my breakfast digesting pretty easy, and found the orders fairly heavy and the kicks rather light, so I told the young man who was reading the mail to me, and who, of course, hadn't had anything special to do with the run of orders, to buy himself a suit of clothes and send the bill to the old man.

Well, when the afternoon mail came in, I dipped into that, too, but I'd eaten a pretty tony luncheon, and it got to finding fault with its surroundings, and the letters were as full of kicks as a drove of Missouri mules. So I began taking it out on the fellow who happened to be handiest, the same clerk to whom I had given the suit of clothes in the morning. Of course, he hadn't had anything to do with the run of kicks either, but he never put up a hand to defend himself till I was all through, and then he only asked:

"Say, Mr. Graham, don't you want that suit of clothes back?"

"Say, Mr. Graham, don't you want that suit of clothes back?"

Of course, I could have fired him on the spot for impudence, but I made it a suit and an overcoat instead. I don't expect to get my experience on free passes. And I had my money's worth, too, because it taught me that it's a good rule to make sure the other fellow's wrong before you go ahead. When you jump on the man who didn't do it, you make sore spots all over him; and it takes the spring out of your leap for the fellow who did it.

One of the first things a boss must lose is his temper—and it must stay lost. There's about as much sense in getting yourself worked up into a rage when a clerk makes a mistake as there is in going into the barn and touching off a keg of gunpowder under the terrier because he got mixed up in the dark and blundered into a chicken-coop instead of a rat-hole. Fido may be an all-right ratter, in spite of the fact that his foot slips occasionally, and a cut now and then with a switch enough to keep him in order; but if his taste for chicken develops faster than his nose for rats, it's easier to give him to one of the neighbors than to blow him off the premises.

Where a few words, quick, sharp, and decisive, aren't enough for a man, a cussing out is too much. It proves that he's unfit for his work, and it unfits you for yours. The world is full of fellows who could take the energy which they put into useless cussing of their men, and double their business with it.

Your affectionate father,

JOHN GRAHAM.

XIII.

From John Graham, at the Union Stock Yards, Chicago, to his son, Pierrepont, care of Graham & Company, Denver.

The young man has been offered a large interest in a big thing at a small price, and he has written asking the old man to lend him the price.

CHICAGO, June 4, 1900.

Dear Pierrepont: Judging from what you say about the Highfaluting Lulu, it must be a wonder, and the owner's reason for selling—that his lungs are getting too strong to stand the climate—sounds perfectly good. You can have the money at 5 per cent, as soon as you've finally made up your mind that you want it, but before you plant it in the mine for keeps, I think you should tie a wet towel around your head, while you consider for a few minutes the bare possibility of having to pay me back out of your salary, instead of the profits from the mine. You can't throw a stone anywhere in this world without hitting a man, with a spade over his shoulder, who's just said the last sad good-byes to his bank account and is starting out for the cemetery where defunct flyers are buried.

While you've only asked me for money, and not for advice, I may say that, should you put a question on some general topic like, "What are the wild waves saying, father?" I should answer, "Keep out of watered stocks, my son, and wade into your own business a little deeper." Though, when you come to think of it, these continuous-performance companies, that let you in for ten, twenty, and thirty cents a share, ought to be a mighty good thing for investors after they've developed their oil and gold properties, because a lot of them can afford to pay 10 per cent. before they've developed anything but suckers.

So long as gold-mining with a pen and a little fancy paper continues to be such a profitable industry, a lot of fellows who write a pretty fair hand won't see any good reason for swinging a pick. They'll simply pass the pick over to the fellow who invests, and start a new prospectus. While the road to Hell is paved with good intentions, they're something after all; but the walls along the short cuts to Fortune are papered with only the prospectuses of good intentions—intentions to do the other fellow good and plenty.

I don't want to question your ability or the purity of your friends' intentions, but are you sure you know their business as well as they do? Denver is a lovely city, with a surplus of climate and scenery, and a lot of people there go home from work every night pushing a wheelbarrow full of gold in front of them, but at the same time there is no surplus of *that* commodity, and most of the fellows who find it have cut their wisdom teeth on quartz. It isn't reasonable to expect that you're going to buy gold at fifty cents on the dollar, just because it hasn't been run through the mint yet.

I simply mention these things in a general way. There are two branches in the study of riches—getting the money and keeping it from getting away. When a fellow has saved a thousand dollars, and every nickel represents a walk home, instead of a ride on a trolley; and every dollar stands for cigars he didn't smoke and for shows he didn't see—it naturally seems as if that money, when it's invested, ought to declare dividends every thirty days. But almost any scheme which advertises that it will make small investors rich quick is like one of these Yellowstone geysers that spouts up straight from Hades with a boom and a roar—it's bound to return to its native brimstone sooner or later, leaving nothing behind it but a little smoke, and a smell of burned money—your money.

If a fellow would stop to think, he would understand that when money comes in so hard, it isn't reasonable to expect that it can go out and find more easy. But the great trouble is that a good many small investors don't stop to think, or else let plausible strangers do their thinking for them. That's why most young men have tucked away with their college diploma and the picture of their first girl, an impressive deed to a lot in Nowhere-on-the-Nothingness, or a beautiful certificate of stock in the Gushing Girlie Oil Well, that has never gushed anything but lies and promises, or a lovely receipt for money invested in one of these discretionary pools that are formed for the higher education of indiscreet fools. While I reckon that every fellow has one of these certificates of membership in The Great Society of Suckers, I had hoped that you would buy yours for a little less than the Highfaluting Lulu is going to cost you. Young men are told that the first thousand dollars comes hard and that after that it comes easier. So it does—just a thousand dollars plus interest easier; and easier through all the increased efficiency that self-denial and self-control have given you, and the larger salary they've made you worth.

It doesn't seem like much when you take your savings' bank book around at the end of the year and get a little thirty or forty dollars interest added, or when you cash in the coupon on the bond that you've bought; yet your bank book and your bond are still true to you. But if you'd had your thousand in one of these 50 per cent. bleached blonde schemes, it would have lit out long ago with a fellow whose ways were more coaxing, leaving you the laugh and a mighty small lock of peroxide gold hair. If you think that saving your first thousand dollars is hard, you'll find that saving the second, after you've lost the first, is hell and repeat.

You can't too soon make it a rule to invest only on your own *know* and never on somebody else's say so. You may lose some profits by this policy, but you're bound to miss a lot of losses. Often the best reason for keeping out of a thing is that everybody else is going into it. A crowd's always dangerous; it first pushes prices up beyond reason and then down below common sense. The time to buy is before the crowd comes in or after it gets out. It'll always come back to a good thing when it's been pushed up again to the point where it's a bad thing.

It's better to go slow and lose a good bargain occasionally than to go fast and never get a bargain. It's all right to take a long chance now and then, when you've got a long bank account, but it's been my experience that most of the long chances are taken by the fellows with short bank accounts.

You'll meet a lot of men in Chicago who'll point out the corner of State and Madison and tell you that when they first came to the city they were offered that lot for a hundred dollars, and that it's been the crowning regret of their lives that they didn't buy it. But for every genuine case of crowning regret because a fellow didn't buy, there are a thousand because he did. Don't let it make you feverish the next time you see one of those Won't-you-come-in-quick-and-get-rich-sudden ads. Freeze up and on to your thousand, and by and by you'll get a chance to buy a little stock in the concern for which you're working and which you know something about; or to take that thousand and one or two more like it, and buy an interest in a nice little business of the breed that you've been grooming and currying for some other fellow. But if your money's tied up in the sudden—millionaire business, you'll have to keep right on clerking.

A man's fortune should grow like a tree, in rings around the parent trunk. It'll be slow work at first, but every ring will be a little wider and a little thicker than the last one, and by and by you'll be big enough and strong enough to shed a few acorns within easy reaching distance, and so start a nice little nursery of your own from which you can saw wood some day. Whenever you hear of a man's jumping suddenly into prominence and fortune, look behind the popular explanation of a lucky chance. You'll usually find that these men manufactured their own luck right on the premises by years of slow preparation, and are simply realizing on hard work.

Speaking of manufacturing luck on the premises, naturally calls to mind the story of old Jim Jackson, "dealer in mining properties," and of young Thornley Harding, graduate of Princeton and citizen of New York.

Thorn wasn't a bad young fellow, but he'd been brought up by a nice, hard-working, fond and foolish old papa, in the fond belief that his job in life was to spend the income of a million. But one week papa failed, and the next week he died, and the next Thorn found he had to go to work. He lasted out the next week on a high stool, and then he decided that the top, where there was plenty of room for a bright young man, was somewhere out West.

Thorn's life for the next few years was the whole series of hard-luck parables, with a few chapters from Job thrown in, and then one day he met old Jim. He seemed to cotton to Thorn from the jump. Explained to him that there was nothing in this digging gopher holes in the solid rock and eating Chinaman's grub for the sake of making niggers' wages. Allowed that he was letting other fellows dig the holes, and that he was selling them at a fair margin of profit to young Eastern capitalists who hadn't been in the country long enough to lose their roll and that trust in Mankind and Nature which was Youth's most glorious possession. Needed a bright young fellow to help him—someone who could wear good clothes and not look as if he were in a disguise, and could spit out his words without chewing them up. Would Thorn join him on a grub, duds, and commission basis? Would Thorn surprise his skin with a boiled shirt and his stomach with a broiled steak? You bet he would, and they hitched up then and there.

They ran along together for a year or more, selling a played-out mine now and then or a "promising claim," for a small sum. Thorn knew that the mines which they handled were no Golcondas, but, as he told himself, you could never absolutely swear that a fellow wouldn't strike it rich in one of them.

There came a time, though, when they were way down on their luck. The run of young Englishmen was light, and visiting

Easterners were a little gun-shy. Almost looked to Thorn as if he might have to go to work for a living, but he was a tenacious cuss, and stuck it out till one day when Jim came back to Leadville from a near-by camp, where he'd been looking at some played-out claims.

Jim was just boiling over with excitement. Wouldn't let on what it was about, but insisted on Thorn's going back with him then and there. Said it was too big to tell; must be taken in by all Thorn's senses, aided by his powers of exaggeration.

It took them only a few hours to make the return trip. When Jim came within a couple of miles of the camp, he struck in among some trees and on to the center of a little clearing. There he called Thorn's attention to a small, deep spring of muddy water.

"Thorn," Jim began, as impressive as if he were introducing him to an easy millionaire, "look at thet spring. Feast yer eyes on it and tell me what you see."

"A spring, you blooming idiot," Thorn replied, feeling a little disappointed.

"You wouldn't allow, Thorn, to look at it, thet thar was special pints about thet spring, would you?" he went on, slow and solemn. "You wouldn't be willin' to swar thet the wealth of the Hindoos warn't in thet precious flooid which you scorn? Son," he wound up suddenly, "this here is the derndest, orneriest spring you ever see. Thet water is rich enough to be drunk straight."

Thorn began to get excited in earnest now. "What is it? Spit it out quick?"

"Watch me, sonny," and Jim hung his tin cup in the spring and sat down on a near-by rock. Then after fifteen silent minutes had passed, he lifted the cup from the water and passed it over. Thorn almost jumped out of his jack-boots with surprise.

"Silver?" he gasped.

"Generwine," Jim replied. "Down my way, in Illinois, thar used to be a spring thet turned things to stone. This gal gives 'em a jacket of silver."

After Thorn had kicked and rolled and yelled a little of the joy out of his system, he started to take a drink of the water, but Jim stopped him with:

"Taste her if you wanter, but she's one of them min'rul springs which leaves a nasty smack behind." And then he added: "I reckon she's a winner. We'll christen her the Infunt Fernomerner, an' gin a lib'rul investor a crack at her."

The next morning Thorn started back, doing fancy steps up the trail.

He hadn't been in Leadville two days before he bumped into an old friend of his uncle's, Tom Castle, who was out there on some business, and had his daughter, a mighty pretty girl, along. Thorn sort of let the spring slide for a few days, while he took them in hand and showed them the town. And by the time he was through, Castle had a pretty bad case of mining fever, and Thorn and the girl were in the first stages of something else.

Castle showed a good deal of curiosity about Thorn's business and how he was doing, so he told 'em all about how he'd struck it rich, and in his pride showed a letter which he had received from Jim the day before. It ran:

"*Dere Thorn*: The Infunt Fernomerner is a wunder and the pile groes every day. I hav 2 kittles, a skilit and a duzzen cans in the spring every nite wich is awl it wil hold and days i trys out the silver frum them wich have caked on nites. This is to dern slo. we nede munny so we kin dril and get a bigger flo and tanks and bilers and sech. hump yoursel and sell that third intrest. i hav to ten the kittles now so no mor frum jim."

"You see," Thorn explained, "we camped beside the spring one night, and a tin cup, which Jim let fall when he first tasted the water, discovered its secret. It's just the same principle as those lime springs that incrust things with lime. This one must percolate through a bed of ore. There's some quality in the water which acts as a solvent of the silver, you know, so that the water becomes charged with it."

Now, Thorn hadn't really thought of interesting Castle as an investor in that spring, because he regarded his Western business and his Eastern friends as things not to be mixed, and he wasn't very hot to have Castle meet Jim and get any details of his life for the past few years. But nothing would do Castle but that they should have a look at The Infant, and have it at once.

Well, sir, when they got about a mile from camp they saw Jim standing in the trail, and smiling all over his honest, homely face. He took Castle for a customer, of course, and after saying "Howdy" to Thorn, opened right up: "I reckon Thorn hev toted you up to see thet blessid infunt as I'm mother, father and wet-nuss to. Thar never was sich a kid. She's jest the cutest little cuss ever you see. Eh, Thorn?"

"Do you prefer to the er—er—Infant Phenomenon?" asked Castle, all eagerness.

"The same precious infunt. She's a cooin' to herself over thar in them pines," Jim replied, and he started right in to explain: "As you see, Jedge, the precious flooid comes from the bowels of the earth, as full of silver as sody water of gas; and to think thet water is the mejum. Nacher's our silent partner, and the blessid infunt delivers the goods. No ore, no stamps, no sweatin', no grindin', and crushin', and millin', and smeltin'. Thar you hev the pure juice, and you bile it till it jells. Looky here," and Jim reached down and pulled out a skillet. "Taste it! Smell it! Bite it! Lick it! An' then tell me if Sollermun in all his glory was dressed up like this here!"

Castle handled that skillet like a baby, and stroked it as if he just naturally loved children. Stayed right beside the spring during the rest of the day, and after supper he began talking about it with Jim, while Thorn and Kate went for a stroll along the trail. During the time they were away Jim must have talked to pretty good purpose, for no sooner were the partners alone for the night than Jim said to Thorn: "I hev jest sold the Jedge a third intrest in the Fernomerner fur twenty thousand dollars."

"I'm not so sure about that," answered Thorn, for he still didn't quite like the idea of doing business with one of his uncle's friends. "The Infant looks good and I believe she's a wonder, but it's a new thing, and twenty thousand's a heap of money to Castle. If it shouldn't pan out up to the first show-down, I'd feel deucedly cut up about having let him in. I'd a good deal rather refuse to sell Castle and hunt up a stranger."

"Don't be a dern fool, son," Jim replied. "He knew we was arter money to develop, and when he made thet offer I warn't goin' to be sich a permiscuss Charley-hoss as to refuse. It'd be a burnin' crime not to freeze to this customer. It takes time to find customers, even for a good thing like this here, and it's bein' a leetle out of the usual run will make it slower still."

"But my people East. If Castle should get stuck he'll raise an awful howl."

Jim grinned: "He'd holler, would he? In course; it might help his business. Yer the orneriest ostrich fur a man of yer keerful eddication! Did you hear thet Boston banker what bought the Cracker-jack from us a-hollerin'? He kept so shet about it, I'll bet, thet you couldn't a-blasted it outer him."

They argued along until after midnight, but Jim carried his point; and two weeks later Thorn was in Denver, saying good-by to Kate, and listening to her whisper, "But it won't be for long, as you'll soon be able to leave business and come back East," and to Castle yelling from the rear platform to "Push the Infant and get her sizzling."

Later, as Jim and Thorn walked back to the hotel, the old scoundrel turned to his partner with a grin and said: "I hev removed the insides from the Infunt and stored 'em fur future ref'rence. Meanin', in course," he added, as Thorn gaped up at him like a chicken with the pip, "the 'lectro-platin' outfit. P'r'aps it would be better to take a leetle pasear now, but later we can come back and find another orphant infunt and christen her the Phoenix, which is Greek fur sold agin."

It took Thorn a full minute to comprehend the rascality in which he'd been an unconscious partner, but when he finally got it through his head that Jim had substituted the child of a base-born churl for the Earl's daughter, he fairly raged. Threatened him with exposure and arrest if he didn't make restitution to Castle, but Jim simply grinned and asked him whether he allowed to sing his complaint to the police. Wound up by saying that, even though Thorn had rounded on him, old Jim was a square man, and he proposed to divide even.

Thorn was simply in the fix of the fellow between the bull and the bulldog—he had a choice, but it was only whether he would rather be gored or bitten, so he took the ten thousand, and that night Jim faded away on a west-bound Pullman, smoking two-bit cigars and keeping the porter busy standing by with a corkscrew. Thorn took his story and the ten thousand back to his uncle in the East, and after a pretty solemn interview with the old man, he went around and paid Castle in full and resumed his perch on top of the high stool he'd left a few years before. He never got as far as explaining to the girl in person, because Castle told him that while he didn't doubt his honesty, he was afraid he was too easy a mark to succeed in Wall Street. Yet Thorn did work up slowly in his uncle's office, and he's now in charge of the department that looks after the investments of widows and orphans, for he is so blamed conservative that they can't use him in any part of the business where it's necessary to take chances.

I simply speak of Thorn as an example of why I think you should have a cool head before you finally buy the Lulu with my money. After all, it seems rather foolish to pay railroad fares to the West and back for the sake of getting stuck when there are such superior facilities for that right here in the East.

Your affectionate father,

JOHN GRAHAM.

XIV.

From John Graham, at the Omaha branch of Graham & Company, to his son, Pierrepont, at the Union Stock Yards, Chicago.

The old man has been advised by wire of the arrival of a prospective partner, and that the mother, the son, and the business are all doing well.

OMAHA, October 6, 1900.

Dear Pierrepont: I'm so blame glad it's a boy that I'm getting over feeling sorry it ain't a girl, and I'm almost reconciled to it's not being twins. Twelve pounds, bully! maybe that doesn't keep up the Graham reputation for giving good weight! But I'm coming home on the run to heft him myself, because I never knew a fellow who wouldn't lie a little about the weight of number one, and then, when you led him up to the hay scales, claim that it's a well-known scientific principle that children shrink during the first week like a ham in smoke. Allowing for tare, though, if he still nets ten I'll feel that he's a credit to the brand.

It's a great thing to be sixty minutes old, with nothing in the world except a blanket and an appetite, and the whole fight ahead of you; but it's pretty good, too, to be sixty years old, and a grandpop, with twenty years of fight left in you still. It sort of makes me feel, though, as if it were almost time I had a young fellow hitched up beside me who was strong enough to pull his half of the load and willing enough so that he'd keep the traces taut on his side. I don't want any double-team arrangement where I have to pull the load and the other horse, too. But you seem strong, and you act willing, so when I get back I reckon we'll hitch for a little trial spin. A good partner ought to be like a good wife—a source of strength to a man. But it isn't reasonable to tie up with six, like a Mormon elder, and expect that you're going to have half a dozen happy homes.

They say that there are three generations between shirt-sleeves and shirt-sleeves in a good many families, but I don't want any such gap as that in ours. I hope to live long enough to see the kid with us at the Stock Yards, and all three of us with our coats off hustling to make the business hum. If I shouldn't, you must keep the boy strong in the faith. It makes me a little uneasy when I go to New York and see the carryings-on of some of the old merchants' grandchildren. I don't think it's true, as Andy says, that to die rich is to die disgraced, but it's the case pretty often that to die rich is to be disgraced afterward by a lot of light-weight heirs.

Every now and then some blame fool stops me on the street to say that he supposes I've got to the point now where I'm going to quit and enjoy myself; and when I tell him I've been enjoying myself for forty years and am going to keep right on at it, he goes off shaking his head and telling people I'm a money-grubber. He can't see that it's the fellow who doesn't enjoy his work and who quits just because he's made money that's the money-grubber; or that the man who keeps right on is fighting for something more than a little sugar on his bread and butter.

When a doctor reaches the point where he's got a likely little bunch of dyspeptics giving him ten dollars apiece for telling them to eat something different from what they have been eating, and to chew it—people don't ask him why he doesn't quit and live on the interest of his dyspepsia money. By the time he's gained his financial independence, he's lost his personal independence altogether. For it's just about then that he's reached the age where he can put a little extra sense and experience into his pills; so he can't turn around without some one's sticking out his tongue at him and asking him to guess what he had for dinner that disagreed with him. It never occurs to these people that he will let his experience and ability go to waste, just because he has made money enough to buy a little dyspepsia of his own, and it never occurs to him to quit for any such foolish reason.

You'll meet a lot of first-class idiots in this world, who regard business as low and common, because their low and common old grandpas made money enough so they don't have to work. And you'll meet a lot of second-class fools who carry a line of something they call culture, which bears about the same relation to real education that canned corned beef does to porterhouse steak with mushrooms; and these fellows shudder a little at the mention of business, and moan over the mad race for wealth, and deplore the coarse commercialism of the age. But while they may have no special use for a business man, they always have a particular use for his money. You want to be ready to spring back while you're talking to them, because when a fellow doesn't think it's refined to mention money, and calls it an honorarium, he's getting ready to hit you for a little more than the market price. I've had dealings with a good many of these shy, sensitive souls who shrink from mentioning the dollar, but when it came down to the point of settling the bill, they usually tried to charge a little extra for the shock to their refinement.

The fact of the matter is, that we're all in trade when we've got anything, from poetry to pork, to sell; and it's all foolishness to talk about one fellow's goods being sweller than another's. The only way in which he can be different is by making them better. But if we haven't anything to sell, we ain't doing anything to shove the world along; and we ought to make room on it for some coarse, commercial cuss with a sample-case.

I've met a heap of men who were idling through life because they'd made money or inherited it, and so far as I could see, about all that they could do was to read till they got the dry rot, or to booze till they got the wet rot. All books and no business makes Jack a jack-in-the-box, with springs and wheels in his head; all play and no work makes Jack a jackass, with bosh in his skull. The right prescription for him is play when he really needs it, and work whether he needs it or not; for that dose makes Jack a cracker-jack.

Like most fellows who haven't any too much of it, I've a great deal of respect for education, and that's why I'm sorry to see so many men who deal in it selling gold-bricks to young fellows who can't afford to be buncoed. It would be a mighty good thing if we could put a lot of the professors at work in the offices and shops, and give these canned-culture boys jobs in the glue and fertilizer factories until a little of their floss and foolishness had worn off. For it looks to an old fellow, who's taking a bird's-eye view from the top of a packing house, as if some of the colleges were still running their plants with machinery that would have been sent to the scrap-heap, in any other business, a hundred years ago. They turn out a pretty fair article as it is, but with improved machinery they could save a lot of waste and by-products and find a quicker market for their output. But it's the years before our kid goes to college that I'm worrying about now. For I believe that we ought to teach a boy how to use his hands as well as his brain; that he ought to begin his history lessons in the present and work back to B.C. about the time he is ready to graduate; that he ought to know a good deal about the wheat belt before he begins loading up with the list of Patagonian products; that he ought to post up on Abraham Lincoln and Grover Cleveland and Thomas Edison first, and save Rameses Second to while away the long winter evenings after business hours, because old Rameses is embalmed and guaranteed to keep anyway; that if he's inclined to be tonguey he ought to learn a living language or two, which he can talk when a Dutch buyer pretends he doesn't understand English, before he tackles a dead one which in all probability he will only give decent interment in his memory.

Of course, it's a fine thing to know all about the past and to have the date when the geese cackled in Rome down pat, but life is the present and the future. The really valuable thing which we get from the past is experience, and a fellow can pick up a pretty fair working line of that along La Salle Street. A boy's education should begin with to-day, deal a little with to-morrow, and then go back to day before yesterday. But when a fellow begins with the past, it's apt to take him too long to catch up with the present. A man can learn better most of the things that happened between A.D. 1492 and B.C. 5000 after he's grown, for then he can sense their meaning and remember what's worth knowing. But you take the average boy who's been loaded up with this sort of stuff, and dig into him, and his mind is simply a cemetery of useless dates from the tombstones of those tough and sporty old kings, with here and there the jaw-bone of an ass who made a living by killing every one in sight and unsettling business for honest men. Some professors will tell you that it's good training anyway to teach boys a lot of things they're going to forget, but it's been my experience that it's the best training to teach them things they'll remember.

I simply mention these matters in a general way. I don't want you to underestimate the value of any sort of knowledge, and I want you to appreciate the value of other work besides your own—music and railroading, ground and lofty tumbling and banking, painting pictures and soap advertising; because if you're not broad enough to do this you're just as narrow as those fellows who are running the culture corner, and your mind will get so blame narrow it will overlap.

I want to raise our kid to be a poor man's son, and then, if it's necessary, we can always teach him how to be a rich one's. Child nature is human nature, and a man who understands it can make his children like the plain, sensible things and ways as easily as the rich and foolish ones. I remember a nice old lady who was raising a lot of orphan grandchildren on a mighty slim income. They couldn't have chicken often in that house, and when they did it was a pretty close fit and none to throw away. So instead of beginning with the white meat and stirring up the kids like a cage full of hyenas when the "feeding the carnivora" sign is out, she would play up the pieces that don't even get a mention on the bill-of-fare of a two-dollar country hotel. She would begin by saying in a please-don't-all-speak-at-once tone, "Now, children, who wants this dear little neck?" and naturally they all wanted it, because it was pretty plain to them that it was something extra sweet and juicy. So she would allot it as a reward of goodness to the child who had been behaving best, and throw in the gizzard for nourishment. The nice old lady always helped herself last, and there was nothing left for her but white meat.

It isn't the final result which the nice old lady achieved, but the first one, that I want to commend. A child naturally likes the simple things till you teach him to like the rich ones; and it's just as easy to start him with books and amusements that hold sense and health as those that are filled with slop and stomach-ache. A lot of mothers think a child starts out with a brain that can't learn anything but nonsense; so when Maudie asks a sensible question they answer in goo-goo gush. And they believe that a child can digest everything from carpet tacks to fried steak, so whenever Willie hollers they think he's hungry, and try to plug his throat with a banana.

You want to have it in mind all the time while you're raising this boy that you can't turn over your children to subordinates, any more than you can your business, and get good results. Nurses and governesses are no doubt all right in their place, but there's nothing "just as good" as a father and mother. A boy doesn't pick up cuss-words when his mother's around or learn cussedness from his father. Yet a lot of mothers turn over the children, along with the horses and dogs, to be fed and broken by the servants, and then wonder from which side of the family Isobel inherited her weak stomach, and where she picked up her naughty ways, and why she drops the h's from some words and pronounces others with a brogue. But she needn't look to Isobel for any information, because she is the only person about the place with whom the child ain't on free and easy terms.

I simply mention these things in passing. Life is getting

broader and business bigger right along, and we've got to breed a better race of men if we're going to keep just a little ahead of it. There are a lot of problems in the business now—trust problems and labor problems—that I'm getting old enough to shirk, which you and the boy must meet, though I'm not doing any particular worrying about them. While I believe that the trusts are pretty good things in theory, a lot of them have been pretty bad things in practice, and we shall be mighty slow to hook up with one.

The trouble is that too many trusts start wrong. A lot of these fellows take a strong, sound business idea—the economy of cost in manufacture and selling—and hitch it to a load of the rottenest business principle in the bunch—the inflation of the value of your plant and stock—, and then wonder why people hold their noses when their outfit drives down Wall Street. Of course, when you stop a little leakage between the staves and dip out the sugar by the bucket from the top, your net gain is going to be a deficit for somebody. So if these fellows try to do business as they should do it, by clean and sound methods and at fair and square prices, they can't earn money enough to satisfy their stockholders, and they get sore; and if they try to do business in the only way that's left, by clubbing competition to death, and gouging the public, then the whole country gets sore. It seems to me that a good many of these trusts are at a stage where the old individual character of the businesses from which they came is dead, and a new corporate character hasn't had time to form and strengthen. Naturally, when a youngster hangs fire over developing a conscience, he's got to have one licked into him.

Personally, I want to see fewer businesses put into trusts on the canned-soup theory—add hot water and serve—before I go into one; and I want to know that the new concern is going to put a little of itself into every case that leaves the plant, just as I have always put in a little of myself. Of course, I don't believe that this stage of the trusts can last, because, in the end, a business that is founded on doubtful values and that makes money by doubtful methods will go to smash or be smashed, and the bigger the business the bigger the smash. The real trust-busters are going to be the crooked trusts, but so long as they can keep out of jail they will make it hard for the sound and straight ones to prove their virtue. Yet once the trust idea strikes bed-rock, and a trust is built up of sound properties on a safe valuation; once the most capable man has had time to rise to the head, and a new breed, trained to the new idea, to grow up under him; and once dishonest competition—not hard competition—is made a penitentiary offense, and the road to the penitentiary macadamized so that it won't be impassable to the fellows who ride in automobiles—then there'll be no more trust-busting talk, because a trust will be the most efficient, the most economical, and the most profitable way of doing business; and there's no use bucking that idea or no sense in being so foolish as to want to. It would be like grabbing a comet by the tail and trying to put a twist in it. And there's nothing about it for a young fellow to be afraid of, because a good man isn't lost in a big business—he simply has bigger opportunities and more of them. The larger the interests at stake, the less people are inclined to jeopardize them by putting them in the hands of any one but the best man in sight.

I'm not afraid of any trust that's likely to come along for a while, because Graham & Co. ain't any spring chicken. I'm not too old to change, but I don't expect to have to just yet, and so long as the trust and labor situation remains as it is I don't believe that you and I and the kid can do much better than to follow my old rule:

Mind your own business; own your own business; and run your own business.

Your affectionate father,

JOHN GRAHAM.

www.ingramcontent.com/pod-product-compliance
Lightning Source LLC
Chambersburg PA
CBHW021147090426
42740CB00008B/986